REPORT

OF A

PUBLIC DISCUSSION

CARRIED ON BY

HENRY TOWNLEY,

Formerly Missionary to Calcutta, and late Minister of Bishopsgate Chapel, London,

AND

GEORGE JACOB HOLYOAKE,

Editor of the "Reasoner," London Periodical, &c.

IN THE

SCIENTIFIC INSTITUTION, JOHN STREET, FITZROY SQUARE, LONDON,

On the Question—Is there sufficient proof of the Existence of a God; that is, of a Being distinct from Nature?

EDITED, WITH NOTES AND AN APPENDIX,

BY HENRY TOWNLEY,

AND A PREFACE BY JAMES BENNETT, D.D.

LONDON:
WARD AND CO., 27, PATERNOSTER ROW.

LONDON:
J. UNWIN, GRESHAM STEAM PRESS,
BUCKLERSBURY.

ADVERTISEMENT.

Toward the close of the past year, the Editor conferred with a venerable and experienced Christian minister, as to the desirableness of some extra effort being made, to commend religion to the more mature consideration of those inhabiting the Metropolis who belong to the sceptical school. He was advised himself, if practicable, to engage in a public discussion, on the being of a God, with one of the leaders of the atheistic body. The result was the debate recorded in the pages of this book.

The speeches were delivered on 24th May and 1st June, 1852, and taken down by a professional reporter. Those delivered by Mr. Holyoake were sent to him by the Editor, with a request that he would revise them for the press. Mr. Holyoake returned the manuscript, regretting that pressing engagements, coupled with ill health, prevented him from effecting the desired revision. His speeches are consequently printed as they came from the reporter's hands.

PREFACE.

We are glad that Mr. Townley has risen superior to the common fashion of considering Atheists to be out of the pale of humanity, and beyond the reach of hope. For though such as still adhere to that opinion may blame him for this publication, as giving currency to what the world had better not know, the reader will perceive that a public contest has elicited, only the weakness of arguments brought against God, the patient reasoning of those who love Him.

Theists have often complained that their difficulty was not to meet arguments against God, but to find them; and the following pages will make many a reader ask, "Where is the argument against God? We have no difficulty in finding here the reason for believing His existence."

It is, however, highly gratifying to observe, that no bitterness, or spite, or ill behaviour, can be charged on either side. This should encourage believers, not merely to hope and pray, but also to labour openly for those who are farthest out of the way of life, and to look for the moment when the God of truth may indulge us with the luxury of saying to our most determined opponent, "Thou art not far from the kingdom of God."

JAMES BENNETT, D.D.

Islington, July, 1852.

CONTENTS.

PUBLIC DISCUSSION

ON

THE BEING OF A GOD.

Mr. SYME opened the debate thus:—I have been requested by the joint-committee to act as umpire in this debate, and I have been requested by the two chairmen to read the rules, which are as follow:—

RULES OF THE DEBATE.

Question:—"Is there sufficient proof of the existence of a God; that is, of a Being distinct from nature?"

Mr. TOWNLEY takes the *affirmative* side.

Mr. HOLYOAKE the *negative*.

The discussion to occupy two hours each evening. Each speaker to have *one hour* allotted to him on the first evening, and alternate *quarters* of an hour on the second.

Mr. TOWNLEY not to be at liberty to introduce any new argument for the being of a God during the final quarter of an hour.

Mr. TOWNLEY to open the debate on the first night; Mr. Holyoake on the second.

Mr. SWAINE to act as chairman for Mr. Townley.

Mr. CLEMENTS to be Mr. Holyoake's chairman.

Mr. EBENEZER SYME to act as umpire.

FIRST SPEECH.

Mr. SWAINE:—It is my simple duty, ladies and gentlemen, now to introduce to you my friend, the Rev. Henry Townley, who is to open the discussion; and all that I have to ask of you is, that he may have that patient hearing which I am sure his friends will accord to Mr. Holyoake. I have only further to express my own hearty good-will to my fellow-men, whatever may be their opinions, and my sincere desire that there should be a fair field for every man.

The Rev. HENRY TOWNLEY:—Mr. Umpire, Chairmen, ladies and gentlemen, I beg to open the present discussion by reading a paragraph contained in a work entitled "The Philosophic Type of Religion, as defined by Professor Newman, stated, examined, and answered," emanating from Mr. Holyoake. The paragraph is as follows:—

"Some modern books which have obtained celebrity in pointing out the errors of popular Christianity, seem to me not to differ from older ones except in amplification of former arguments, now urged with more decorousness than was formerly the case, because the subsidence of dangerous persecution has left room for the manifestation of the gentlemanly tone; but there is no more *feeling* displayed in the efforts than before. The critical surgeon has removed the diseased part, or perhaps amputated the limb very cleverly, and taken his fee of public applause as a skilful operator; but he has displayed no personal sympathy with his patient. In Mr. Newman's case it is altogether different. He never forgets that his patient is his brother. You may feel pain under his hand, but you are persuaded his is the hand under which you will suffer least, and that his affection and intelligence will save you all he can. He is the friend, and never the opponent. He does not offend you by spiritual superciliousness. There is no tone of pride about him. There is no lie for the glory of God in him; he does not recognise that God can be glorified by any word of deceit. To disparage, to mortify, to obtain a victory over you, are pettinesses of controversy which he despises. He is never angry, petulant, or harsh. He never plays the priest—soft and gracious when his argument opens, menacing, imperious, and contemptuous when it closes without being accepted. His profound respect for others, for their sincerity and well-meaning, is uninterrupted. Yet in all this gentleness there mingles no weakness. Every affectionate word is animated by a masculine strength of will, and in this union of both qualities, a great lesson in intellectual and moral strength is afforded. No man, whether believer or atheist, can read this book without great improvement, unless he be very good indeed, or entirely incapable of moral appreciation."

I cannot but regard this as a beautiful description of the temper which every disputant,—every religious disputant, in particular,—ought to display. To my mind, it is the *beau ideal* of a polemic. I thank Mr. Holyoake for it. I hope to profit by it; and intend to keep it in view, as the model for my own imitation, throughout the present controversy.

I beg to read an extract from a work, also proceeding from the pen of the same author, but upon a different topic; the

title is, " A Logic of Facts ; or, Plain Hints on Reasoning."
The paragraph reads thus :—

"Common sense is the substratum of all logic; common sense is the
natural sense of mankind. It is founded on common observation and experience. It is modest, and plain, and unsophisticated. It sees with everybody's eyes, and hears with everybody's ears. It has no capricious distinc-
tions, no partialities, and no mysteries. It never equivocates, and never
trifles. Its language is always the same, and is always intelligible. It is
known by its perspicuity of speech, and singleness of purpose. The most
prudent of all the children of fact, it never forsakes nature or reason. Ever
dwells this power with the people. How great would be their influence
were this power but methodised."

As the first paragraph describes the spirit which I desire
to breathe in this debate, so the mode in which I desire to
argue is suggested in the second. I thus intend, while this
controversy is in progress, that love shall be the feeling of
my heart, the language of my lips shall be that of truth and
common sense.

I now proceed to the question :—" Is there sufficient
proof of the existence of a God; that is, of a Being distinct
from nature ?"

In order to avoid future obscurity and misapprehension, I
beg to make a few preliminary remarks upon the phraseology
and design of the question. By the term " nature" I understand, matter with its properties, together with life, mind,
and instinct seated in matter with their properties ; all matter—the entire universe. " A Being distinct from nature"
I regard as a *preternatural* Being, in whose essence there is
no matter, and no life, mind, and instinct seated in matter.
The meaning of the term " God" is defined in the question ;
it is there declared to signify " a Being distinct from nature:" I consequently understand it as intending " a Being
in whose essence there is no matter, and no life, mind, and
instinct seated in matter—a preternatural Being."

I understand the term " God" as also signifying a *supernatural* Being ; that is, a Being above nature, as well as distinct from it—and I do so in harmony with the definition in
the question ; for superiority over nature rather augments
than destroys distinctness from it. I am thus explicit
because I may often have occasion to use the term " supernatural," and wish it to be clearly understood, that when I
do so, I mean to *include*, not to exclude, what is *preternatural.*

I would further observe, that the term "God" is defined in the question—and purposely so defined—as not meaning exclusively *one* solitary Being. The question is not worded thus—Is there proof of the existence of " *God*," but of " *a God*,"—a phrase suited to plurality as well as to unity; for if there is but one God there is a God, if there are more than one there is still a God. This wording was not accidental, but intentional; it being deemed a more likely way of arriving at truth, to take up the question of the existence of the Deity *in its most elementary form*.* If it be established that there is "a God," then a good basis will have been laid for discussing, at a future time, the question of the Divine *Unity*.

I make a similar observation with regard to the *infinitude* of God. The term " God" is so defined in the question— and studiously so defined—as not to mean exclusively an *infinite* Being; the question is not worded thus—" Is there proof of the existence of God, that is, of an *infinite* Being distinct from nature ; but, of a God—a Being distinct from nature ?"—a phrase suited to limitation as well as boundless- ness in the Divine attributes. It will not, therefore, devolve upon me to offer any proof either of the unity or the infinity of the Godhead.

As to the expression, "sufficient proof,"—" Is there *suffi- cient proof* of the existence of a God ?"—it may be under- stood in two senses : first, "proof sufficient to render it probable that there is a God," such probability being the

---

* Mathematicians commence their solutions with the most simple and elementary problem which it is in their power to construct. Having succeeded, they proceed to one less simple ; and then advance, step by step, till they have solved problems the most difficult and complicated. So ought theologians to act. The first problem for theologians to solve is, " *Is there a Being distinct from nature, a Deity of any kind ?*" To discuss what kind of Being the Deity is, till it is ascertained that a Deity of some kind exists, is unphilosophical, and tends to prevent the dis- covery of truth. If reason give a negative reply to the above primary ques- tion, all further theological research must obviously be labour in vain. If, on the contrary, the answer of reason be affirmative, a basis is evidently laid for subsequent gradual inquiries respecting the unity, the infinitude, the attributes, the manifestations, the acts and the purposes, and other matters respecting the Deity. According as an inquirer disposes of the *primary* question, so he pertains either to the theistic or atheistic school. The great *fundamental* difference between the Theist and the Atheist is, *that the Theist believes there is a Being distinct from nature, a Deity of some kind ; the Atheist believes that there is no Being distinct from nature, no Deity of any kind.*

basis of belief, and calling for it; in this sense I understand the expression. It may also mean, "proof sufficient to render it important to pursue a religious course;" I accept of this meaning also, and understand it in each of these two senses.

It will therefore be incumbent on me, taking the affirmative side of the question, to adduce proof of the existence of a *preternatural* or *supernatural* Being—of a God distinct from nature—proof sufficient to produce both faith and practice.

I remark, further, that proof sufficient to call for religious practice need not be so strong as that which calls for faith; because, in matters of practice, especially in important affairs, prudent men often act upon proofs and reasonings too weak to produce probability. For instance, if a very advantageous post become vacant, a man will try to obtain it, though the chances be fifty to one against his success; he acts upon an *improbability*. If a man be the proprietor of a valuable house, and it constitute the whole of his property, though it may be a thousand to one, and more, against his house being destroyed by fire, yet, to be on the safe side, as a prudent man, he will be at the trouble and expense of going annually to a fire-office, and paying a premium that his house may be insured. So, should a man deem the proof of the existence of a God to be so weak as to render it improbable, very improbable, that there is a God before whom, after death, he will have to appear, yet prudence will dictate to him the propriety of pursuing such a religious course on earth, as will turn out most to his advantage in the world to come, in the event of what now appears very improbable, hereafter turning out to be actual matter of fact.[b]

That a Divine Being exists, there are many proofs—some derived from Scripture, some from sincere and earnest Theists, some from geological phenomena, some from nature at large. From these I select the proof arising from the supernatural

---

[b] *Probability* as to result, is the chief guide, the polar star of human conduct. The instances in which a man acts with a *certain* foreknowledge as to result, are comparatively of rare occurrence. Whilst a wise man, in some cases, acts upon *improbability* as to result, it is never in the way of exposing himself to danger; but it is either for the purpose of protecting himself against some great possible calamity, or of gaining some great possible good.

organisms which are visible in nature, such organisms being the basis of what is commonly called " the design argument."

The argument which I employ, arising from these organisms or organizations, I would state in two propositions, which, if established, will lead to a conclusion requiring an affirmative answer to be returned to the question which is now before us.

First proposition:—IF THERE BE IN NATURE THE MANIFESTATION OF SUPERNATURAL CONTRIVANCE, THERE MUST EXIST A SUPERNATURAL CONTRIVER.

This proposition is not stated absolutely, but hypothetically.

By " supernatural contrivance," I mean a contrivance beyond the power of any human being, or of any other being in nature, to produce. By " supernatural contriver," I mean—in harmony with the remarks which I previously made—a Being as well *distinct* from nature, as superior to it ; a Being answering to the definition given in the question of a God.

Second proposition:—THERE IS IN NATURE THE MANIFESTATION OF SUPERNATURAL CONTRIVANCE.

There is the manifestation of a contrivance beyond the power of any human being, or of any other being in nature, to produce.

If I can succeed in establishing these two propositions, this conclusion inevitably follows—

THEREFORE, A SUPERNATURAL CONTRIVER (that is, a God) EXISTS.

With regard to the first proposition, "If there be in nature the manifestation of supernatural contrivance, there must be a supernatural contriver,"—a contriver out of nature,—a contriver distinct from nature. The truth of this proposition, I apprehend, cannot, and will not be disputed. It is, in fact, *a truism.* To deny the truth of it would be to assert a contradiction in terms ; for the term contrivance affirms a contriver, by whom it was produced ; the same as the term husband affirms a wife to whom the husband has been married. The word contrivance carries, within itself, the declaration that there is a contriver ; as the word husband carries, within itself, a declaration that there is a wife.

The term " contrivance" affirms also an *adequate* contriver, for an inadequate contriver cannot be a contriver.

An inadequate contriver is not equivalent to a contriver—it is quite a different thing; a counterfeit sovereign is not a sovereign, but something essentially differing from it.

The term "supernatural contrivance," for a similar reason, affirms "a supernatural contriver."

I proceed now to consider the second proposition,— "There is in nature the manifestation of supernatural contrivance."

The establishment of this proposition, as it seems to me, does not involve much difficulty. Common sense, having made its common observations, will, I think, substantiate the proposition, by affirming the three following truths :—

First.—That in nature there is the manifestation of contrivance of SOME SORT.

No man, I apprehend, after observing the human eye, the human ear, the hand, the foot, the various organs in the human body, will affirm, that in all these there is no manifestation of any contrivance whatever. Common sense will affirm, that there is the manifestation of contrivance of some kind.

Second.—That in nature there is the manifestation of SUPERHUMAN *contrivance*—such contrivance as no man, or number of men, could produce.

Common sense, observing the exquisite and wonderful structure and organism manifested in trees and plants— fishes and birds, beasts and insects—in the human body, its bony skeleton, muscles and ligaments, nerves, limbs and joints, arms and legs, brain, veins and arteries, eyes, ears, hands, feet, and other organs—common sense, observing such organisms as these, cannot but declare that man is utterly unequal to their production.

Third.—That in nature there is the manifestation of SUPERNATURAL *contrivance*—a contrivance which not only no man could produce, but to the production of which no other being in nature is equal.

Let it be observed, that all the contrivances which have been named, all the organisms to which allusion has been made, have been produced *on earth?* There is no natural contriver *upon earth* adequate to their production. Man is at the head of natural contrivers upon earth, and it has been shown that he cannot produce such contrivances. Hence it necessarily follows, that *they can be produced by no natural*

contriver whatsoever.   Therefore, to a supernatural contriver,
acting upon earth, they must be ascribed.   Now, that which
none but a supernatural contriver can effect, is a supernatural
contrivance ; and thus the second proposition, that there is
in nature the manifestation of *supernatural* contrivance, is
established.

The conclusion follows, as a matter of course, *there is a
supernatural contriver—a Being distinct from nature—there
is a God.*

Perhaps it may be asked, has not Mr. Holyoake, in his
work entitled " The Logic of Death," given such a view of
nature as is sufficient to produce a reasonable belief that
there is in nature *superhuman* intelligence, and thus got
rid of the objection to which atheism stands exposed,—that
of inability to find an intelligence sufficient to produce the
various contrivances which nature exhibits to our view ?

To Mr. Holyoake's views of nature, as recorded in " The
Logic of Death ; or, Why should the Atheist fear to die ?"
I will now refer ; they appear in the following paragraph :—

" It is not in a low, but in an exalted estimate of nature that my rejection
of the popular theology arises.   The wondrous manifestations of nature
indispose me to degrade it to a secondary rank.   I am driven to the conclusion that the great aggregate of matter which we call 'nature' is eternal,
because we are unable to conceive a state of things when nothing was.   There
must always have been something, or there could be nothing now.   This
the dullest feel.   Hence we arrive at the idea of the eternity of matter.
And in the eternity of matter we are assured of the self-existence of matter,
and self-existence is the most majestic of attributes, and includes all others.
That which has the power to exist independently of a God, has doubtless the
power to act without the delegation of one.   It therefore seems to me that
nature and God are one—in other words, that the God whom we seek is the
nature whom we know.

" I will not encumber, obscure, or conceal my meaning with a cloud of
words.   I recognise in nature but the properties of matter.   The term
God seems to me inapplicable to nature.   In the mouth of the Theist, God
signifies an entity, spiritual and percipient, distinct from matter.   With
Pantheists, the term God signifies the aggregate of nature—but nature as a
being, intelligent and conscious.   It is my inability to subscribe to either of
these views which constitutes me an Atheist.   I cannot rank myself with the
Theists, because I can conceive of nothing beyond nature, distinct from it,
and above it.   The language invented by Pope, expressing that ' we look
through nature *up* to nature's God,' has no significance for me, as I know
nothing besides nature, and can conceive of nothing greater.   The majesty
of the universe so transcends my faculties of penetration, that I pause in
awe and silence before it.   It seems not to belong to man to comprehend its
attributes and extent, and to affirm what lies beyond it.   The Theist,

therefore, I leave; but while I go with the Pantheist so far as to accept the fact of nature in the plenitude of its diverse, illimitable, and transcendent manifestations, I cannot go farther and predicate with the Pantheist the unity of its intelligence and consciousness. This is the inability, rather than any design of my own, which resolves me as one of that class of speculationists designated, in the technicality of theology, Atheists."

The question now arises, Does Mr. Holyoake here assert the existence of a *superhuman* contriver? If he do not, nothing that he has advanced will affect my argument. It seems to me, (he will correct me, if I prove in error,) that such assertion he does not make. I will examine those parts of the statement which bear upon the point. The following is one of them:—"And in the eternity of matter we are assured of the self-existence of matter; and self-existence is the most majestic of attributes, and includes all others." Here all attributes are ascribed to matter,—of course, intelligence will be included. But then, observe, *the extent of these attributes is not intimated.* It is not said that these attributes surpass those which are human. Superhuman intelligence is, therefore, not here attributed to nature.

But, then, it may perhaps be said, that the words which immediately follow imply that superhuman intelligence is to be found in nature. · The words are, "That which has the power to exist independently of a God, has doubtless the power to act without the delegation of one. It therefore seems to me, that nature and God are one,—in other words, that the God whom we seek is the nature whom we know." Superhuman intelligence might seem here to be predicated of nature; but then, these words are revoked by what immediately succeeds: "I will not encumber, obscure, or conceal my meaning with a cloud of words. I recognise in nature but the properties of matter. The term, God, seems to me inapplicable to nature."

There is yet a remaining clause to be noticed. "But while I go with the Pantheist so far as to accept the fact of nature in the plenitude of its diverse, illimitable, and transcendent manifestations:"—If these manifestations are ascribed to illimitable intelligence, then, of course, there is the assertion of which we are in quest; but the words which follow throw a considerable amount of doubt whether that be the due interpretation. "I cannot go farther and predicate with the Pantheist," Mr. Holyoake adds, "the unity of its intelligence and consciousness." He cannot predicate the *unity* of intelligence in matter. His inability so to predicate implies his belief in *the distribution or diffusion of intelligence amongst the component parts of matter.* Man is one of those component parts, and, of course, he has his share; his share we have found not to be enough, we require more intelligence than man possesses. Thus nature, even as described by Mr. Holyoake, does not possess superhuman intelligence, and we have it yet to seek.

I will suppose, now, for argument's sake, that I have misunderstood Mr. Holyoake, and that he meant to ascribe to nature a superhuman intelligence. Can it, I ask, be proved that nature is in possession of it? Nature consists of countless millions of particles of matter, capable of being separately considered. Does any single particle of matter contain that which we seek—superhuman intelligence? No one will affirm it. Do millions of particles possess it? Common sense answers, No. A million, or any assignable number of things, each one of which is individually destitute of intelligence, will also collectively be destitute of it.

It may now, perhaps, be asked, does not Mr. Holyoake, in his work entitled "Paley's Natural Theology refuted in his own Words," bring forward proofs and arguments, which will overthrow one or both of my propositions? I think he does quite the contrary. He appears to me virtually to admit the truth of my propositions, and of my conclusion also.

The proposition, that "if there be contrivance in nature there must be an adequate contriver," seems to be admitted in page 19, the first line in which reads thus:—"That design implies a designer I am disposed to allow." Design, here, is not used in opposition to contrivance, but in unison with it. It is a concise mode of referring to the argument, which includes both contrivance and design. Designer means an adequate designer. If design or contrivance be supernatural, the designer or contriver must be supernatural also. I therefore regard this as virtually admitting my first proposition to be true.

The proposition, that "there is supernatural contrivance in nature," is also virtually, in its primary element, admitted, in page 26, where it is written:—"We shall find

that organization proves contrivance. There is no organization which does not manifest contrivance." This admission, I think, substantially recognises the fundamental point
in my second proposition. But I hasten to observe, that
everything my argument goes to prove, and all which in
this debate I endeavour to establish, is admitted in page 10,
where the author says:—" Hume pointed out that all *à
posteriori* reasoning must fail to establish the existence of
Deity. And had he pointed out *how*, with Paley's force
and fulness, there would have been little occasion for this
work. Hume's words are these:—'It follows that the
argument *à posteriori* only leads to the conclusion, that a
finite, and not an infinite, or an indefinitely wise and powerful Being exists! But there are few persons who would
feel all the force of the remark, from the barren statement
given of it.'"

It is quite clear, that Hume's view is approved by Mr.
Holyoake. And Hume admits, that by " *à posteriori*
reasoning," that is, by the design argument, a finite Deity
is proved to exist.

There is one other quotation which I must notice. It is
in page 37:—" If natural theologians were content to stop
where they prove a superior something to exist, Atheists
might be content to stop there too, and allow theologians to
dream in quiet over their barren foundling." I cannot
interpret this language otherwise than as meaning, that if
Deists would behave themselves properly, and not push
matters too far—if they would not go ahead of reason, the
Atheist would accompany them up to the point of admitting
that a superior something does exist.

I promise to be on my good behaviour, and not to push
matters unreasonably far,—by no means to shoot ahead of
common sense ; therefore I pray our friend to declare absolutely and unhesitatingly on this platform what, in his book,
he has admitted in a manner somewhat conditional and
undecided.

I may now be permitted to state, as bearing upon the
question in debate, that Mr. Henry Knight declares that
he has been of late much exercised in his mind respecting
his disbelief in the existence of a Divinity, and that he
has at length come to the conclusion that his atheistic
views had no solid basis on which to rest, and is resolved

publicly to declare that he now believes there is a God. This has not arisen from any intercourse with myself (for I was never in his company till yesterday), but from his own researches and reflections.

I was made acquainted with Mr. Knight's altered views on Friday last, on which day he favoured me with the following communication :—

"REV. SIR,—I am doing an act which plunges me at once into the most abject poverty. I must bear it.

"By the blessing of God, the exercise of those mental powers which He has bestowed upon me, has led me to the conclusion that 'He' exists. There is a God.

"The mystery of the God-man Jesus is no longer a mystery to me. Christianity is an everlasting truth. I have prayed to God through Jesus Christ, and I am happier; and but for the past——but I have a hope now, which for years I have not had.

"Go on with your good work; and pray, as I will, that 'He' may pardon the ignorance of all, and show them, as 'He' has shown me, that atheism is a convulsive struggle to escape from the acknowledgment of an incontrovertible fact.

"Your obedient Servant,

"4, Claremont-place, Pentonville,   "HENRY KNIGHT.
    Friday, May 21st, 1852.

"Read this publicly—print it—publish it in any way; and God's blessing be with it and you.

"HENRY KNIGHT."

"To Rev. HENRY TOWNLEY."

What joy it would give me if he who is now taking the atheistic side of the question before us, would reconsider and renounce his present opinions also. I have perused all his works of which I could obtain copies with great interest. I have read the affecting narrative he gives of his prosecution, trial, and imprisonment; and must confess that my sympathies were not with the prosecutors, but with the prisoner; and I feel as though I should have been glad to have stood bail for him on the occasion; and I must add, that if he should be called to account by the Attorney-General for truly and fearlessly uttering all that is in his heart to-night, I would ask him as a favour to let me subscribe towards the expense of his defence.

I perceive that the hour allotted to me is rapidly drawing to a close. Before it expires, I wish to refer to the celebrated atheistic work, entitled, "The System of Nature: or, the Laws of the Moral and Physical World;" ascribed, in the title-page (though perhaps erroneously) to M. de Mirabaud. Some might be ready to ask, "Has not this able and eloquent French philosopher placed atheism upon a firm and immoveable foundation? Have I courage enough to attempt to answer the arguments against theism which have been adduced by him?" I reply, that to answer the writer of "The System of Nature" is quite unnecessary; for he has sufficiently answered and refuted himself. In his work, to which I have referred, he writes as follows :—

"The great CAUSE OF CAUSES must have produced everything; but is it not lessening the true dignity of the Divinity to introduce him as interfering in every operation of nature,—nay, in every action of so insignificant a creature as man,—as a mere agent, executing his own eternal, immutable laws; when experience, when reflection, when the evidence of all we contemplate, warrants the idea that this ineffable Being has rendered nature competent to every effect; by giving her those irrevocable laws, that eternal, unchangeable system, according to which all the beings she sustains must eternally act? Is it not more worthy the exalted mind of the GREAT PARENT OF PARENTS, *ens entium*, more consistent with truth to suppose, that his wisdom, in giving these immutable, these eternal laws to the macrocosm, foresaw every thing that could possibly be requisite for the happiness of the beings contained in it; that, therefore, he left it to the invariable operation of a system, which never can produce any effect that is not the best possible that circumstances, however viewed, will admit."

There are several other passages in the "System of Nature," to the same effect. The writer of it reminds me of a modern anonymous production, entitled, "Vestiges of the Natural History of Creation;" the author of which does not impugn the belief that there is a God, but simply objects to the supposition that God occasionally interposes, and by the special exercise of his attributes brings new kinds of creatures into being.

The writer of the "System of Nature" seems to take precisely the same view as the author of the "Vestiges of Creation." He uses the very term, *Divinity*; and he speaks of this Divinity as *giving laws to matter*, which implies that he is *distinct from matter* to which he dictates.

Had time sufficed, I would have read passages contained in other books now on the table before me. I would have read some of the sayings of Locke, of Voltaire, of Thomas Paine, of the ancient and sagacious Greek philosopher, Socrates, and others.[c] But I must forbear : and I now sub-

---

[c] See Appendix A.

mit, that I have advanced proof enough to carry my point ; that neither of the propositions which I have laid down can be overthrown; that the preponderance of the argument will appear to be on my side—for if what can be urged against the existence of a Deity should be regarded as having the strength of fifty, less a fraction—and what can be said in favour of his existence be accounted as fifty and a fraction[d] — in such case, the existence of a Deity is probable, and the question in debate must receive an affirmative reply.

It will, then, be further obvious, that there is more than a sufficiency of proof to render it a matter of prudence, to lead such a life in this world as will best conduce to our well-being in the world to come; for happiness is what is needed—perfect happiness is what I seek. I possess it in element, I have enjoyed the foretaste of it, and I wish every one here present—especially Mr. Holyoake—to share it with me. I am admonished my hour has now expired.

---

[d] The proposition, "There is a Being distinct from nature,—a Deity," may be regarded in five different lights. 1st. As *certainly* true. 2ndly. As *probably* true. 3rdly. As *doubtful* respecting its truth. 4thly. As *probably* untrue. 5thly. As *certainly untrue*. A view of the proposition as *certainly true* arises from *such an amount of evidence in its favour as is equivalent to the demonstration of its truth*, and produces *knowledge*. A view of it as *probably true* arises from a *preponderance of evidence in its favour*, and produces *belief*. A view of it as *doubtful* arises from the *evidence on both sides being equal*, and produces *scepticism*. A view of it as *probably untrue* arises from a *preponderance of evidence against it*, and produces *disbelief*. A view of it as *certainly untrue* arises from *such an amount of evidence against it as is equivalent to the demonstration of its untruth*, and produces *knowledge*. *Some Theists* view the proposition as *certainly true*. *Some Theists* view it as *probably true*. Few, if any, view it, at least for any length of time, as *doubtful;* because a small matter will turn the scale. *All intelligent Atheists* view it as *probably untrue*. *No intelligent Atheist* views it as *certainly untrue;* for before he could reasonably regard it in that light, he must have explored not only the entire universe, but all space lying beyond it, to satisfy himself, from ocular inspection, that nowhere any trace or footprint of a Deity is to be seen. If, in the scale for the existence of a Deity, there be evidence equivalent to fifty and a fraction; and in the opposite scale evidence equivalent to fifty, less a fraction; then the preponderance is in favour of the existence of a Deity, and the proposition cannot be regarded either in the first, third, fourth, or fifth point of view, but in the *second* only ; it must necessarily be regarded as *probably true;* and, with an *equal necessity,* the question in debate must be answered in the affirmative.

SECOND SPEECH.

Mr. CLEMENTS:—Ladies and gentlemen, I have now to introduce to you Mr. Holyoake, and have only to request of you the same impartial hearing that you have given to Mr. Townley. I do not request this from any doubt in my own mind, but as a mere matter of form, for your conduct hitherto leads me to believe that it will be continued as it has been begun.

Mr. G. J. HOLYOAKE:—We shall all be indebted to the very fair manner, and to the genial and considerate spirit in which Mr. Townley has laid his case before us this evening. He might have done what so many are accustomed to do—invoke those prejudices which always surround the consideration of this question, and prevent any impartial examination of it. As he has not done so, he ought to be credited with a desire to have this matter tested exclusively by such logical properties as do, in my opinion, seem to belong to it.

The aspect in which persons view the side which I take, is not always favourable to anything like a calm consideration of such reasons as we are accustomed to adduce for the negative nature of our opinions upon this question. I should, in propitiation of such apprehensions, say that, though upon this matter I take what is called the negative side, it is not because I have no positive view with regard to it—it is not because I have not a positive end in view, in what I am doing. It seems to me that, when we assert that a certain case is not proved, the assertion is entered upon in order to establish something else, which we suppose to be better, in its place, and which we would substitute for that.

I therefore accept the position here of affirming a negation; I do it in obedience to the logical argument of the proposition which has been put before you. I should, on any other occasion, tell you that none of us, I believe, ever make an objection to that which we suppose to be error, without having before us, either distinctly portrayed or dimly shadowed, something which we believe to be right—something which we think is the truth, and which already we have some glimpse of, and contrasted with error already existing. It is because we would vindicate that sort of truth, that we at any time undertake the task of giving a negation to that which we suppose to be error.

Why do I appear to speak, as I do now, against that presumption of common sense to which Mr. Townley has very properly referred? It is because the case is my own. We have had, to-night, no indication of anything that lies beyond the mere proposition as to whether a Being exists independently of nature; but neither of us would take an interest in a controversy on this point, if it were not for the foregone conclusions upon it—that this Being, distinct from nature is in possession of certain attributes which are of immense consequence to us, if established. It is because there is more mixed up with the question than the mere fact as to whether some Being exists independently of nature; for instance, if any man would debate whether there existed a Divine Being—whether a Providence, who was the father of his creatures, whom we could propitiate by prayer in our danger, from whom we could obtain light in darkness, and help in distress—if any man debated a proposition like this, I should say there was much of great practical utility about it; I presume, the only value of debating it in this form is that afterwards that might come out of it.

If you tell me God exists, that he is a power, a principle, or spirit, or light, or life, or love, or intelligence, or what you will; if he be not a father to whom his children may appeal—if he be not a Providence whom we may propitiate, and from whom we can obtain special help in the hour of danger—I say, practically it does not matter to us whether he exists or not. When I say practically, I do not say it in a disrespectful spirit, as to whether it was perfectly ideal or not, but I say it with respect to the great business of life ; and if I supposed that the Christian world meant no more by it than this reverend gentleman inferred to-night—that something exists independently of nature, that it may be boundless, that it may be limited, that it may be one, that it may be many Beings—if I supposed nothing more than that was meant, then surely I would not occupy your time, or my own, in discussing a question so barren of practical consequences.

My friend implied more in this indication when he said

it was prudent for us to believe peradventure on what, under other circumstances, might be an insufficiency of evidence; he admonished us about prudence, because certainly there must be some danger in the question as to whether we hold this opinion or not. If he had no danger in the background which he was then foreshadowing, he would not have used the word " prudence," and have told us it was prudent to believe, in order to protect ourselves against what may be consequences of a serious nature. Speaking advisedly as he did, he would not have used that term, unless there was connected with it much more than appears in the present proposition; and if I did not believe it was so connected, I would not stand here, and debate this question.

I say I will inform you of the spirit in which I approach this matter. Persons are very apt to overlook that what we believe—the opinions which we hold—are matters of personal consequence to every man; that he may be able to walk by the light he may have; but it is my business to take care, if I walk from time to eternity, that I walk by that light which satisfies my own understanding.

If it were true that any of you would take my place—if we should eventually find ourselves at the bar of God, about whom we are just now discussing, and I should find myself to be made answerable for the opinions which I entertain, or for beliefs which I had in time—if any of you, or all of you, would take my place, and answer for me, then I might be content to take your opinions, then I might stand on the side of the world; but what does it matter to me what Newton believed, what Locke believed, or what the world believes, unless the world will answer for me if I believe as the world believes?[*]

I am as much concerned as this reverend gentleman can be, as to what shall be the issue of my own condition in the future; I am as much concerned in the solution of this question as he is himself; and I believe that the view I en-

---

[*] " Quote others," says Mr. Holyoake, in his " Logic of Facts," "as Grotius di:d not as judges, from whose decision there is no appeal, but as witnesses, whose conspiring testimony confirms the view taken." I thus quote others as witnesses to confirm the view I have taken; and such witnesses are entitled to a hearing, even though they do not make themselves answerable for the sins of those who listen to their testimony.

C

tertain, or that any of us may entertain, conscientiously, will be our justification in that issue, if we should come to want justification. When we pass through the inexorable gates of the future; when we pass through that vestibule where Death stands opening his everlasting gates as widely to the pauper as to the king; when we pass out here into the dim mysteries of the future, to confront, it may be, the interrogations of the Eternal—I apprehend every man's responsibility will go with him, and no second-hand opinions will answer for us. Nothing can justify us, nothing can give us confidence, but the conscientious nature of our own conclusions; nothing can give us courage but innocence; nothing can serve our turn but having believed according to the best of our judgment, and having followed those principles which seem to us to be the truth.

I therefore say, in the language of one of those thoughtful modern Germans, "What I hold to be the truth shall be welcome to me, let it sound as it may; but I will know, and should this be impossible, thus much at least I will know, namely, that it is not possible to know."

I presume, that in the argument to which we have already listened it is hinted, that it is intended that we should know something. The purport of this controversy, so far as it has been at present conducted—and perhaps we cannot make all the use of it which a more ample opportunity might have enabled one to do, because I am somewhat in the position of those Apostles, not by the way of gifts, but by need of gifts, of whom it is said, in a certain hour when they shall need certain things, it shall be given them what they shall say. As I could not foresee what our friend would say, or what I had to reply to, I certainly stand in need equally of having gifts as to what I should say adequately and pertinently to this subject.

But, foreshadowed as we have had the question in the speech which has been delivered to us, it has gone on the assumption—and I attach importance to it—it has gone on the assumption, not that there has been an appeal simply to our faith, not a very important appeal to our prudence, not an appeal to our apprehensions and our fears, so much as an appeal to our reason.

The supposition this gentleman has made surely is this—that he presents certain arguments to us which would satisfy

us to a considerable extent; if they did not give us absolute
certainty, they should give us some comparative assurance,
and awaken in us such confidence in the truth of the propositions he has established, that we shall be able to found our
practice upon it, and, as he hopes, our faith also. I say, therefore, supposing this should be the case, I was at the outset
very much concerned with the definition or explanation which
he gave of the sense in which he understood the matter—in
which he understood the terms of the proposition which we
are to debate. Really, it seems to me that the proposition
is one that cannot be maintained upon the foundation on
which it is sought to make it rest—that there does exist a
Being independent of nature, and that that Being, as I understood, is a Being supernatural and above nature. Why, it
seems to me that it is necessary, if that Being be not nature,
have none of the attributes of nature, none of the will or
desires or passions of nature—if it be so clearly removed
from what we call nature or matter as has been laid down,
it is to me very evident that this world will not at any time
retreat into the assumption of the Pantheist, that nature is
also God; but he intended to maintain throughout that
there is a Being existing independent of nature, having none
of its attributes, distinct from it, and not to be confounded
with matter. That implies something inconceivable, I think,
in the eye of reason; we find it difficult to get out of the
association of time. If I understand it, it is an immense
supposition, it involves that this Being — and how are
we to account for nature at all, unless we are to account
for something?—he does intend to account for contrivance by the agency of this Being distinct from nature—
but if this Being, distinct from nature, is unlike nature,
and also the author of nature, then nature cannot be regarded as any extension of his own being, but as a distinct
production—as something he has created by the *fiat* of his
own will.

I say, I can understand what is meant by that—the assertion is clear enough; but who can make plain to human
reason an act like that of creation? Who can make plain
to us that there could, by possibility, be an act performed
like that? We are brought at once to a Being whom we
cannot conceive of, and who must be the subject of hypothesis, for the understanding cannot repose upon it, the

senses cannot repose upon it, we cannot define it to one
another, we cannot tell what sort of a Being this is, for we
must express all the attributes by a negation of matter, and
we must suppose it without the properties of matter, we must
suppose it without the attributes of matter, yet capable of
doing that of which we have no conception, namely, bringing
this vast frame of all things out of nothing.[c]

Now I submit that only as a difficulty which affects the
understanding of the matter. If the proposition had been
taken—as it is usually taken by theologians in this day—
that it is also a matter of faith as well as of reason—if the
assumption was not to make this plain to the understanding,
then it would be different; but the assumption of the
speaker, the assumption of the proposition is that plainly
this act has been performed. How can that be explained to
us, and made conformable to reason, which we are so incapable of comprehending in any form or degree? I maintain
it is useless to talk about probabilities in this case—about
there being forty-nine or fifty upon the one side, and fifty
and a fraction on the other; here there is nothing in favour
of such a supposition that nature itself is the work of creation, because the more we dwell upon the theory, I conceive, we find we must come to the conclusion that what is
always must have been, or must have come from nothing,
and that we cannot comprehend—we may put it down as a
matter of faith, but we cannot classify it among the victories
of reason.

You will permit me to say a word upon the manner in
which the nature of this Being was itself described,—that it
might be plural as well as one, or the terms implied one, or
it might be limited; and there was a reference made to an
admission of mine that the design argument, carried out,
legitimately established the existence of a limited being.
Very well; I grant that my friend was right in supposing I
should be as frank in my speech as I have been in my book,
and that I am willing to allow that, so far as the design argu-

---

[c] I never alleged that the argument I employed was intended to prove
that God created the universe, or any part of it, out of nothing, but only
to prove *the existence of a Deity of some kind*. Whether God is the
Creator as well as the organizer of matter is a question very proper to be
considered *after* the existence of a Deity has been established.

ment goes, it establishes a Being which is distinct from nature—of limited nature; but that is not the Being of which we are in search. We reason in this proposition to find a Being distinct from nature, who can also be the author of nature, who can be the cause of nature, who can be adequate to all that exists; but if we find by reasoning on the design argument that we come to a Being that exists, that is limited, defined, and has power not adequate for the performance of that which we find in nature, then we discover our search has been in the wrong direction,[d] it does not end advantageously to us, and we have to renew[e] our inquiries, because, if we are to come to the words of the controversy, if it does not matter what we believe in, if it does not matter what kind of a Being we establish by argument, it does not matter that we argue at all about it. We never can disassociate from the issue of this discussion the nature of the Being we establish by it. If we suppose for one moment that we can disassociate it from the inquiries, we condemn the inquiries, and expose ourselves to the objection made frequently against inquiries, that these are merely speculative and merely trifling.

I feel anxious to fully justify myself before so large a number of persons, who choose to give a night to the consideration of this question, against the supposition that I would for one moment occupy myself with anything less than a direct practical issue. I deal with this question—I trust we shall always have it so treated—I deal with it on strict practical grounds. It does not concern me to put any gentleman in the wrong—that some parties believe wrong; it does not concern me to announce this fact, or put certain believers on the wrong side,—I am not concerned to put them in the wrong, but to put myself and others in the right; I am anxious for something to come out of this issue which shall be of service to us, for we have somewhat endangered our controversy—the advantage of free speech—by not always taking care, when so many persons are inclined to protest against that privilege, not to

---

[d] It is not a search in a wrong direction to begin with the great fundamental and primary inquiry, " Is there a Deity of some kind ? "

[e] In the event of a Deity being discovered, we have not to renew, we have to *extend* our researches.

employ it on that which is speculative, barren, beyond time, and therefore obscure; but we should take care to employ it upon that which goes home to men's business and bosoms, and gives them something on which they can repose, and by which they shall better direct their lives.

Turning to the nature of the arguments which were advanced, they seem to me to be of two descriptions principally—the strength of analogy, the presumption of likelihood—the sort of common consent with which people look over nature, and ascribe to nature the presentment of instances which must have been the work of a supernatural Being; as I understood the argument, it took these two forms. First, of the great probability of the thing, from the close inspection of it, that matter being incapable of doing all the things which are presented to us, and also of the necessity of calling in the supposition that a Being distinct from nature had done all those things, and that the design argument, even as he himself had explained it, had admitted that the design had a designer, that this designer was God, though he might be a limited Being—that was asserted, and that was sufficient for the purpose.

I will treat first of the matter of probability. My own impression is, we do not know enough about nature to be able to say nature is incapable of doing what is evidently manifest to us is a work of nature.[f] I commonly find that the pervading theological notions regard nature very much in the light of an intelligent tool of Deity—a sort of instrument whereby things are done; and all that glory, and all that beauty, and all that intense interest with which nature is otherwise invested, it seems to me nature is deprived of by this representation, and that the view of the Pantheist is far nobler, far more inspiring, which reads in nature the revelation of God himself.[g]

But the assumption is, we may look through nature up to nature's God. That seems to me to imply a power, a capacity, an endowment, which repels me at the outset. If we are to deal with the common sense of probability, I say I am repelled by the amazing probability which is against

---

[f] A mill grinds corn, but common sense declares it to be *incapable* of action, excepting in an *instrumental* sense; it being devoid of the intelligence requisite to *efficient* agency.

[g] The Theist reads in nature the revelation of God himself.

me if I am to deal with the assumption of distinctness—that I can look from nature up to nature's God. Why, in the presence of this shadowy form of things, before which all men stand in awe and dread—in the presence of so many mysteries and marvels which art is unable to unravel, which science is unable to unravel, which philosophy is unable to explain, it seems to me an immense endowment,[b] when a man can say with confidence, I look through nature and beyond nature up to nature's God. I say, the presumption of the thing does repel me, and I have as much right on my part to consider what is unlikely, to consider what is unreasonable, what ought to offend, I think, the just modesty of nature, as those friends, on the other side, to consider what in my theory may offend their own presumption of theories, or their own proprieties of reason.

I think that when we come to ascribe so much incapacity to nature, where there is nothing beyond this probability by which we can try the question, we very much overlook how often we mistake the first impressions which we receive, and even the peculiar impression mankind may get during a long period of the contemplation of nature.

I remember observing, in the case of a little boy with whose instruction I was charged, that when he made some overtures of a playful nature to a strange cat, she only returned them by scratching him, and he asked why it was. He was told the cat was strange, and when she knew him better she would treat him more kindly. Some time after, a Parisian lamp, which he never saw before, was introduced into the house where he was. Owing to the unskilfulness of those who had the use of it, it did not burn, and he asked this question, "When the lamp is used to us, then will it burn?" His assumption was that the lamp had personality; like the cat, had its own antipathies; and would not burn because it did not know us, and was not used to us. This, with extreme simplicity, will illustrate what I believe has taken place in the infancy of the world: with regard to the presumption about nature, men are no better informed than the little boy,—the things he observed gave him the impression that there was, and must be, personality every

---

[b] It is only a common endowment to be able from effects to infer their efficient causes.

where.[1] The whole experience of this I have put in these words :—

" So soon, in the infancy of the human race, that animal wants were satisfied, and man walked forth to meditate, he would be struck with the phenomena of nature and the obvious order of its extempore manifestation, and ask, 'What does all this mean?' In the roar of the ocean, the rush of blast, the gloom of the night, and the beam of the sun, he would see the rage and strength, and frown and smile of nature. Analogy, the specious precursor of reason, would suggest the personality of the powers which awed and cheered man. Reason sends us to facts as the only positive ground of positive conclusions; but in the childhood of intellect and experience, *likelihood* is mistaken for *certainty*, and *probability* for *fact*. In the distorted reflection of man's image on the wall, as it were, of the universe, arose the idea of gods. The same analogy which gave them birth and invested them with consciousness, suggested their propitiation. Hence arose idolatry, the first form of worship. This was the *origin* of religion. And it is a strong suspicion against its philosophic truth, that its origin was in the infancy of intellect, and that in every succeeding stage of mental growth, men have questioned its soundness more and more.

" Yet this very idolatry was truer than the instinct of orthodoxy, as idolatry recognised the supremacy of nature. The dawning

'————————————————— Mind
Saw God in clouds, and heard him in the wind.'

" Idolatry deified the universe; orthodoxy degraded it by setting a rule over it. The savage theologians erred in inferring the consciousness of nature. Unsophistication led them right, naturally and inevitably, in acknowledging nature to be the source of life. It was analogy which led them wrong (in personifying the material influences as gods) and gave birth to orthodoxy."

Now, it seems to me that in that manner, first of all, arose those various impressions which induced us to ascribe to nature a personality of power, and afterwards they were removed to a Being beyond the clouds, because it was discovered, by the operation of science, that many of those secondary causes, which men only were able to observe, were

---

[1] Those who consider nature as producing human eyes, ears, hands, feet, and such-like organs, resemble the little boy who, in the first instance, ascribed personality to the lamp. But in the same way as the child (subsequently instructed by the plenary testimony of its senses) would, in due time, cease to regard the lamp as possessed of life and personal endowments, so men, in the infancy of the world, might have been led to regard nature as possessed of superhuman intelligence and other lofty attributes; but hearkening to the reiterated and continually increasing testimony of their senses they would, in due time, regard nature in the light of unintelligent materials, wrought upon by some living agent possessed of intelligence sufficient to bring such materials into the organic forms which they display.

to be traced to material agency, and then the idea of God retreated, retreated from Polytheism into Unitarianism, and Theism has placed the idea of Divinity as being altogether removed from nature.[k]

If we test the matter of probability—if we try it by our common consciousness—this is the account which, I think, properly may be given of the operations of nature. What is the solution to which we can come, is out of the pale of this controversy. My own impression is, that nature is self-existent, nature is eternal, nature is material. I mean by materiality, or by matter, that which is calculable by laws,[l] that which has a certain calculable procedure—it is that method of nature which we observe and describe and calculate. It seems to me, the nature we know is all that is meant by the theological phrase of "the God which we seek"—that it is sufficient by its own power of existence. If we reason about it, unless we take refuge in the idea of a creation which we cannot understand, we must come to the conclusion that nature is self-existent,[m] and that attribute is so majestic—the power of being independent of any ruler, the power of being independent of the law[n] of other

---

[k] The Divinity is regarded as a Being distinct from nature, but not as "beyond the clouds," not as "altogether removed from nature," but as *present with it.*

[l] Nature *is* ruled by laws; *this,* reason will not deny; this, reason will loudly affirm; and as laws ruling and coercing a subject necessarily imply a lawgiver distinct from the subject ruled and coerced, so the laws which rule and coerce nature necessarily imply a lawgiver who rules and coerces nature. *Such a lawgiver to nature is but another name for Deity.*

[m] A thing existing and continuing to exist when such thing never began to exist, is more inconceivable than the performance of a creative act. For reason can conceive of the existence of an Almighty Being; and having done so, can conceive of that Being performing any act not involving a contradiction; but reason cannot conceive of continuance without commencement. Reason is here, as in many cases, constrained to believe that to be true as to *fact,* of which it can form no conception as to *mode.*

[n] Matter is evidently *not* independent of law (see the last note but one); and as the master is more noble than the servant, the high probability is that the great lawgiver who controls matter takes precedence of matter with respect to *antiquity* as well as authority. Reason revolts at the thought of thus addressing a single particle of unintelligent matter— "O thou ancient of days, thou great Eternal!" and what it cannot say to one particle, it cannot say to a multitude of particles, however numerous, however cohering, or however arranged, they may be. But to address such language to nature's lawgiver, reason feels no repugnance, but, on the contrary, is instinctively inclined.

beings, seems so majestic as fairly to be supposed to include all others, for that which has power to be has power to act; for the power to be is the most majestic of all forms of action.

The next form which the argument took was that which had relation to common sense; and in the extract read from "The Logic of Facts," a description was brought to your notice of how common sense is the substratum of all objects. So it is; the first impression of men is undoubtedly proper to be respected; that which common sense declares to be truth is to be regarded differently, and is to be examined; but when I said common sense was the substratum of logic, it merely implies, though it was the beginning of logic, it was not the end of it. If we look over the nature of our own impressions, we find we always shall begin with things which lie below reason—with things plainer than reason—with things which need no demonstration. Such is the nature of the human mind, that we all begin in this sphere of equal knowledge, we begin under the dominion of the senses, and whatever comes within that wants no demonstration, wants no proof, wants no logic—it is the constant, it is the most indubitable, it is the most indisputable of all our knowledge; and if the question of the being of a God came within that sphere—if it was found amongst those indisputable truths—if it was found to be a matter of sense, then there would be no occasion for us to reason at all about it; it could not be a matter of controversy, because it never would be a matter of dispute.

What we mean by logic is, that art, that contrivance in which we express our truths, in which we collect that which is known together, and promulge it, and bring that which is unknown and conjectural, and place it, as it were, by the side of light and intelligence, in order that it may diffuse the light of nature which is known, over the sphere of philosophy and conjecture which is unknown. And we do this, and when we—not as a test, for logic is the test by which we try our consciousness—logic is the test by which we establish that—that is the reason why there are so many opinions in the world, and so many theories in favour of which you may invoke the strongest conclusions of common sense; but at last they have been given up, when they come to be tried by experience; when they come to be tried, one by one, by fact ; when they come to be tried by calculations which we understand—when we put a question of facts on the one side, and all we can get on the other, in order to see on which side the great probability of truth is.

An argument derived from the general consent of mankind has, indeed, a great presumption in its favour; but there is, at the same time, a presumption against it, since the generality of men are ignorant. Certainly, many beliefs have been universal, which are now almost universally discredited.

What Dr. Johnson said of the universal belief in the existence of ghosts, may be applied to the assumed universal belief in Deity :—

"That dead men are seen no more, I will not undertake to maintain against the concurrent and unvaried testimony of all ages and all nations. There is no people, rude or learned, among whom apparitions of the dead are not related and believed. This opinion, which perhaps prevails as far as human nature is diffused, could become universal only by its truth. Those, that never heard of one another, would not have agreed in a tale, which nothing but experience can make credible. That it is doubted by single cavillers can very little weaken the general evidence ; and some who deny it with their tongues, confess it by their fears."

I bring forward this instance, because it is the first, the strongest, the most conclusive proof ; and it suggests to us how frequently the conclusions of what is called common sense—how frequently those conclusions have to be rectified by experience, to be tried by fact, and to be revised by philosophy.

You will, therefore, understand, it involves no serious contradiction on my part—that I am disposed to say, that we are at perfect liberty to reconsider whatever common sense may make apparent to us, with a view to determine whether or not we have the right notions about it ;° that is the practical purport of all the controversies in which we engage.

You heard distinct reference made to the argument of design. The great force of what our friend said, briefly amounted to the improbability of matter being equal to the production of the various things we observe in nature.

We are curious to account for those things, and when I cannot account for them by one process which the theologian

---

° See the eighth speech.

may point out, then I have to look in some other direction
to account for them.   Why I suppose nature is equal to the
performance of all things is, not because the matter has a
certain form, and does not do certain things now—if the
world could wait *long enough*,[p] if time were given sufficient
for the purpose, we should find that this matter would change
without help on our part, and would become we know not
what, because it has already become what it is from what we
are not able to explain.   We look at it, and call it inanimate
because it continues in a set form, and of a certain nature;
but there is nothing in the world, so far as we know, that is
not subject to change, and does not seem by its own innate
power to become at one time or other various beings, and
present various phenomena of contrivance which we, refusing
to allow it to be the work of any power of our own, ascribe
to the work of a Being distinct from nature.

The most eminent person who has done this has been Dr.
Paley.   Now, Dr. Paley tells us, that design proves a designer.   When I made the admission, I was going in the
footsteps of Paley, and adopting his own phraseology; then
I came to his conclusion to see whether it was right, and
then I gave it up—when I found it led me to a contrary
result, then I gave it up; what I supposed to be design in
the opening of my argument is no longer design.   My
reverend friend is wrong in supposing that I admit design,
and yet refuse to admit the force of the design argument.
Paley says :—

"Design proves a designer—a designer a person—a person an organization—and contrivance proves a contriver," (I quote Paley).   "Whatever
includes marks of contrivance whatever in its constitution testifies design,
necessarily carries us to something beyond itself.   No animal, for instance,
can have contrived its own limbs and senses; can have been the author to
itself of the design with which they were constructed.   That supposition
involves all the absurdity of self-creation, that is, acting without existing."

Now, my objection to this theory is briefly this—that it
involves a Maker of that Maker also, and from the fitness of
the world to the end, they infer the necessity of an intelligent Creator.   The argument is, that if I see design, for

---

[p] Here reason is disregarding the testimony of common sense, and lis-
tening to that of mere conjecture.   (See the eighth speech.)

instance, in the human hand, I must suppose it the work of a designer, because I cannot otherwise suppose how it came, unless it was the work of a designer. Why cannot I suppose it might be the work of nature? Because, they say, we never saw nature perform an act of that kind—we have no experience in nature that there exists any power to produce the design which the human hand may manifest. If any one could show an experience in favour of the design of the human frame being the work not of a designer, then the argument would fall to the ground. If you apply the same principle, it involves that which renders the argument utterly useless, because a contriver is insinuated in the beginning, to account for contrivance—so we want a contriver to account for that contriver in the end. If design must have had a designer, because everything in nature put together by contrivance is design, then we know that the contriver of nature must also have had an organization,[q] and we know the contriver must be a person. Paley says, the contriver of nature must be a person, just as the contrivance of all things in works of art are contrived by a person, because, if you do not allow the contriver of nature must be a person, you make out nothing, because, if not a person,—then I do say, if the designer of nature is not a person,[r] why need not the designer of nature be nature itself? If we are not obliged to have a person, we may accept nature; unless design is the work of a person, it may be the work of nature. If we show it cannot be the work of a person, because wherever there is the work of a person there must be organization, you cannot conceive of a person without organization. My friend supposes he can, but if he tries to describe a person without organization, he can give you no distinct idea—he will give you no designer whatever.[s] If the designer of nature is a person, and has organization, it must manifest itself in marks of contrivance, for the reasoning of

---

[q] After much research, I have not been able to discover a shred of evidence calculated to prove that my argument, grounded on supernatural contrivances, establishes the existence of an organized Deity. (See the fourth and sixth speeches.)

[r] See the fourth speech.

[s] In order to a belief that an unorganized Deity *exists* merely, it is by no means necessary to possess a previous description of such Deity. The existence of a force called gravitation is believed to exist, though a des-

all this school is—when we look through nature, we find the
more intellectual the performances—the term being used in
comparison with animal—the more intellectual is the organization of the man, whereby he performs them among the
human family.   Observe, then, they come to the conclusion
that the designer of nature must have been greater than
man. So he must, no doubt, and his organization must be, by
parity of reasoning, if we are to follow it; and if we are not
to follow reason in the end, I do not know why we should
follow it in the beginning.   If we do follow it to the end, it
comes to this—that the designer is a person, that person has
organization, that organization must have had contrivance,
that contrivance must have had a contriver, and then the
Deity you have found for yourselves was not the author of all
things—an absolute Being, because there must have been a
Being beyond him who created him, and who could not have
been created by the Deity you have found.

The argument of my friend is, that I object to him for
carrying the conclusion too far; my objection is the contrary—they do not carry it far enough; they stop short in
the midst of their chain of reasoning, which would bring
them to a conclusion they did not intend to come to—my
complaint is, they do not go far enough.   He said he would
be on his good behaviour, and stop where I wished. I
wished him to go on, not to stop, but to carry the conclusion
right out.

Now there is upon the face of this a presumption against it,
and I would suppose, having this work before him, that my
reverend opponent would have applied himself to the points
which I have myself indicated in the book, where, if there be
weakness, its weakness will be sure to appear. If I have no
right to carry out that analogy, they are right, and I am
wrong.[t]   Have I a right, when they say the designer must
be a person, to say he must, if he be a person, have organi-

cription of such force be not given. The existence of an unorganized
Deity is known in the same way that the existence of the force called
gravitation is known—namely, by such visible effects having been produced as cannot be accounted for but upon the hypothesis that such invisible cause exists.

  t *Mr. Holyoake has carried out no analogical argument at all, but
fallen into a fundamental error as to the mode in which analogical
reasoning is conducted.* (See the sixth speech.)

zation ?ᵁ They do not carry it out—I do, and I am justified
in doing it. My answer to them is this—if you carry
design in nature to a designer, you do it because you find the
design in art and manufacture proceeds from a person ; if
you reason from what you know to prove the designer of
nature must be a person, I have a right to reason from what
I know to prove that, like other persons, he must have
organization. Then we go on to the issue that the organization must manifest contrivance, and above all we see that
that must imply a contriver, and then you have a series of
beings rising in gradation one above another. But that
which you set out to discover—the contriver, the author of
all things, the one Supreme Being, one person, or unity,
which should have been of all power and might and majesty,
the author of all things, I say your mode of reasoning brings
you not to that conclusion, and that fact is not established.ᵂ
The ground upon which I put this is, that we are not
here to reason from Scripture, not to reason from matters
of faith, but from what are called the probabilities of reason.
I say it is of no use to set out on a road, unless that road will
bring us to the end of the journey ; and if we set out to
prove the author of all things, we have a right to expect
the road we take will lead us to that conclusion ; if it does
not, we come backˣ and say we have not found the satisfaction we desire, and therefore we must come to the conclusion
the case cannot be made out, or that is not the way by
which it can be made out—we must take other means, and
I am sure that is not the way it can be made out. Professor
Newman, from whose work Mr. Townley quoted, has himself

ᵁ Mr. Holyoake has no logical right whatever so to say (see fourth
speech), and *even if he had such right, it would not at all affect my
argument,* in which (as the phraseology of the question at issue requires)
the term "being," and not the term "person," is uniformly employed.

ᵂ Mr. Holyoake has here overlooked the one simple intention of the
debate, which is, to obtain an answer to the question, "Does any Divinity
of any kind exist ?" A deeply important and vital point, and which,
in a controversy between Theists and Atheists, ought to have priority of
consideration, and to be settled in the affirmative, before any other question is entertained. (See remarks upon the question in debate, at the commencement of the first speech.)

ˣ If we find that we have travelled the first stage of our journey in a
right direction—if we have reached the point of discovering that a God of
some kind exists—we need not retrace our steps, but we should, on the
contrary, *press forward,* till we have reached our journey's end.

pointed out the unsatisfactory nature of that argument, and so many people have given it up in all sorts of schools, that not one time in twenty a reverend gentleman will recur to it.

There are other modes of much more importance, which require far more accuracy of thought to deal with than this, which is the broad mechanical argument, not brought to perfection by Paley, and which is now disused among cultivated theologians and metaphysicians,[7] too cumbrous to be employed, and involving fallacy so palpable[8] that it makes no impression on the common understanding when we see through the application of it.

I justify myself for this brevity in the matter, because we are not to forget there are many persons here who have been in possession of a better argument, who will think I have not established my case. You will not find me assuming that I have established my proposition, because I have answered yours, or a dozen more. I know how much lies beyond, and how much has to be considered; but what I should be able to establish, if I went over all, would be this:—if we mean to set out to get satisfaction—if we are to get satisfaction for the understanding, we have a right to expect it before we sit down. If you do as the philosophers tell us, you have no right to satisfaction, your understanding must be in abeyance, we must call up the intelligence of the heart, we must call up aspiration, we must have faith, that is a different question; and the position of those whom they call speculatists or disbelievers is, we take this question—can it be made out by reason? If it cannot, then I say that the serious practice which is founded on it is not justified.

My friend tells me, that though the probability may be small, yet men found their practice on small probabilities. He tells us of persons who, though there may be fifty chances against them, go and endeavour to get a place; but if the persons did not know beforehand that there was a place to be got, they would not go at all.[9]

---

[7] I possess no evidence that the statement here made is sustained by fact. As far as my knowledge extends, the reverse is the case.

[8] Fallacious in the view of those only who misapprehend the *real nature* of the argument grounded on the supernatural contrivances which nature everywhere displays. (See the first and eighth speeches.)

[9] Mr. Holyoake is completely in error in supposing that I assumed the

When a man goes and insures his house against fire, it is because he knows that fires do frequently happen, and he has seen them; but if he had never heard of a fire, except from the declarations of the pulpit—if he had never heard of a fire, except when portrayed in sermons—you would have no Insurance Associations. I say, as a proof of this, although we have been told, for 2,000 years, about eternal fire, we have not a single Insurance Society against it.[b] If I had as clear a conviction of the truth of this doctrine as pulpits preach of—if I was as sure as those Christians are who dissent from what I say, then would I not hesitate to say, that it would be perfectly possible to mark out the true path to any man; and he might on earth assure himself, with certainty, as to eternal salvation. I say, the probabilities are not such as our friend describes. That is the whole amount of the argument I employ; but there is this wide dissimilarity between the two cases, as to human experience. It proves the cases are not so well established, as in this moral case he has brought before our notice, and put to suggest that the probabilities were as great in favour of eternal security as moral security.

I will only mention one fact, beyond adverting to Mr. Knight's letter. When that was read, there were some persons who uttered a manifestation, which I was sorry to

---

existence of a place of eternal happiness. I merely assumed, and that *for argument's sake alone*, that if a man paid practical attention to his well-being in the eternal world, it was fifty to one against such attention issuing in any beneficial result; and then, reasoning from the conduct of prudent men respecting their temporal interests, suggested that man's eternal well-being was so great a good, that it would be acting wisely to seek it, though the improbability of success should be regarded as great.

[b] Mr. Holyoake is again entirely in error in supposing that I assumed the existence of eternal punitive fire in the unseen state. I merely assumed, and that *for argument's sake alone*, that if a man paid no practical attention to his preservation from evil in the eternal world, it was a thousand to one against such neglect terminating in any disastrous result; and then, reasoning from the conduct of prudent men respecting their temporal interests, suggested that man's protection from an eternal calamity was of so high importance, that it would be acting wisely to seek such protection, though the improbability that any eternal calamity would ever be experienced was exceedingly great. Let me take up Mr. Holyoake's metaphor, respecting an Insurance Society, and say, with mingled faith and joy, that a GREAT AND ACCREDITED ACTUARY has actually come from the eternal world to this, *to protect against eternal risk all, without exception, who are willing to accept his guarantee.*

hear; because, if the gentleman has been with us, he will respect the good of us generally. It was not my good fortune to know if he held our opinions; and, if he no longer holds them, we ought to take care so to behave ourselves, that he shall be sorry that he has left us, rather than glad that he .has withdrawn from us, that he may have no reason to regret that he ever belonged to us. The better course is to listen with patience to what Mr. Knight shall say, if ever he should favour the world with the reasons which made him what is called—if he ever did call himself—a believer. If he will favour the world with the reasons which induced him to disbelieve, and to come to a different conclusion, then we shall all profit by it. The letter gives us .no information beyond the fact that he saw differently; but what he saw before is not communicated, therefore we have only to listen respectfully. We are in no way informed, or able to judge.

The last thing that I have to say is, the argument of prudence, to which our friend referred in his opening, is one of great importance. If it be prudent for us to be believers, irrespective of evidence whereby we may be guided, or if it be prudent in us to make sure, in that case it must be only on the supposition that we must believe, or ought to believe, though the balance in favour of belief should be very little, because, if it be a matter of prudence, there may be odds against us.

Now I think *that* the demoralization of reasoning. I know, on the part of my friend, this is said in the utmost purity—this is said in kindness, to warn us against what he supposes may be a precipice: but I submit, in human affairs we never so act; and a man never asks himself, whether it is safe and proper to be a patriot, or to take the side of truth—he only asks, not whether it is prudent, but whether it is his duty to do so—whether it be right and proper. I confess, I believe in this matter we ought to disregard the question of prudence, and cleave closely to the reasons of our conduct, and to the righteousness of our actions.[c]

---

[c] My belief is, that no man acts a truly prudent part who does not do his duty, and that no one ever truly does his duty who is inattentive to the voice of prudence. Genuine prudence and genuine virtue I regard as at once inseparable companions and mutual help-mates.

I will only add, I differ from my friend. I cannot say, with my friend, I am in search of happiness. I think, happiness ought to be a secondary thing. Our first thing is to make sure we are right; the next thing, is to make sure we do our duty. It is our business to walk in the right path, and leave our happiness to take care of itself. Harm can never happen to any who believe only that which seems to be true, who do only that which seems to them to be right, and who walk uprightly among men. Such people do not require prudence; prudence is best answered by that course, and happiness will come in the end.

The UMPIRE:—You will allow me to say, that the discussion stands adjourned till Tuesday, the 1st of June, at a quarter past eight o'clock. I have to thank you, on behalf of myself, the chairmen, and the disputants, for your attention to-night.

Mr. CLEMENTS:—Ladies and Gentlemen,—Mr. Syme, the umpire, has not arrived yet, but it is considered that we shall behave ourselves so well that we can go on without him. In introducing Mr. Holyoake again to your attention, I have only to request that you will keep that order which the seriousness of the subject demands.

THIRD SPEECH.

Mr. HOLYOAKE:—As I happen to be suffering from a troublesome cold, I am afraid that I shall trespass somewhat on your patience, in consequence of the deliberateness with which I must speak.

It falls to my lot to open the discussion this evening. There is no more for me to do than to suggest some of the difficulties which lie in the way of the solution of the subject under consideration, in the manner in which the Rev. Mr. Townley proposes to afford us a solution of it.

It would not be possible for me, in the short space of fifteen minutes, to do much in the way of explaining what views on the whole I entertain upon the other side of the question; I shall concern myself, therefore, chiefly with the consideration of the validity of his own case. Briefly I may indicate my notion of the impossibility of defending the proposition which is under discussion, namely, the existence of a Being independent of nature; and when I heard, the last evening of the discussion, the letter read of Mr. Henry Knight, telling us of his conversion, I felt disposed to say that it would not be difficult to show one of two things— either that that gentleman never had any proper reasons for being what he professed to be when he lately lectured in this place, or he has no proper reasons for being what he now is. I mention that as indicating the absolute sort of conviction which I entertain with regard to the possibility of establishing a proposition like that of the existence of a

Being which should be independent of nature, and independent, too, of all natural attributes. It seems to me, before such a proposition can be proved, we ought to be informed of the manner of the existence of such Being. With respect to all existences which are hidden from our senses—which do not appeal to us in the form of any physical fact—there is no mode, I believe, whereby any person can establish the reality of such existences, without explaining to us the manner of the existence of such beings.[a] How is any person to explain the manner of the existence of a Being who, to speak plainly, must have no manner at all? For if he have none of the attributes with which we are conversant in the contemplation of what we call nature, it must be a difficult and almost impossible thing for any person to explain to us what can be the nature of that Being's existence; and unless the manner of existence, which is hidden from us, is satisfactorily explained, I believe it is not possible for us to identify such existence in our understanding; and unless we can so identify it, how shall we know that that independent Being of which we speak is the cause of the various phenomena for which we have to account? If we cannot tell the manner of the existence of such a Being, for all we know some other Being, of whose manner of existence we are equally ignorant, may be the cause of all those existences.

Now, the processes by which these arguments are usually conducted are of this kind—they all proceed by analogy; except in one or two attempts of the *à priori* mode of reasoning, which now are very seldom repeated, and have never been found satisfactory, they all proceed by analogy,[b] with the view of explaining to us how, by the similitude of one kind of action, we may possibly come to judge of the certainty of the existence of some agent independent of nature.

Sometimes we are referred, as we were referred last week,

See note s, page 29.

[b] The argument with which I commenced, and upon which I have throughout relied, is not constructed according to the process of analogical reasoning, but in harmony with the *inductive* mode (see page 6.) As Mr. Holyoake inadvertently confounded Paley's argument by analogy with the argument by induction (see the sixth speech), so he has here and elsewhere inadvertently confounded my argument by induction with that which is carried on by analogy.

to the doctrine or theory of design; but if we, as was then pointed out, follow up that mode of reasoning upon the principle of analogy, or likeness, or similitude, on which it rests at the outset—if we follow it out to the conclusion—it is inevitable that we should be led, by the contemplation, to the consideration and the admission of an infinite series of beings,[c] utterly dissimilar in kind from the first cause of all existence, which it is the purpose of all these controversies to seek.

Sometimes we are told that this independent Being is an intelligence, sometimes a power, sometimes love, sometimes light, sometimes a spirit. But we know, if we apply the term intelligence in any strictness, all we know of intelligence is, it is matter of growth and development. We have no idea of intelligence distinct from some form of personality, and it has also the peculiarity of being a thing of growth and development, which would be inapplicable to any idea of a first intelligence or the great cause of all things.

Now, all power is a mere attribute of matter. We are not able to conceive of a power as distinct from some form or other of matter, by which we get the impression of power or capacity of overcoming resistance.

Now even love itself is but a form of affection, and must have, I presume, some personal and material being, in which even that affection itself can reside. Light has its own conditions, and seems—as we know it to be—a sort of calculable manifestation; seems to have, also, its own material source, its own material condition. So one might go through the whole of the possible things on which human ingenuity, at various times, hath fixed attention, and show, by what we call analogy—by the getting of one thing from another—that these all lead us away from the solution of which we are mainly in search.

If we say it is a spirit—as I suppose my friend here would tell us—a spirit seems to me, what he has formerly told us his conception of this independent Being is, the negation of all matter. Now that which is the negation of all matter is, in fact, but another form of giving up the question so far as explanation can carry it; it is but another form of saying—Really, I cannot tell what it is.

The reason why it presents this aspect is, that when a

---

[c] See the sixth speech.

man departs from the attributes with which he is but very imperfectly acquainted, and proceeds to say that a Being in whom he believes, is entirely distinct from all the attributes of matter, I say it is not possible, after that declaration, to explain to us what the nature of the Being is of whom he speaks.

Now you will say it is presumptuous in me to expect to have this matter explained, and that I am pushing the argument of the satisfaction of the understanding too far. But the nature of my difficulty is this—I do not present it as a reason why I am unwilling to believe as you would have me believe, but I am assigning the cause why I am not able to adopt your hypothesis. The purpose for which we reason is that we may understand the matter. If you tell me that a Being, who has none of the attributes of matter—that a Being, of whom you can give no possible account—is the cause of all things, I ask, why may not nature, of whom we can give some account, be the cause of all things?

Now, the manner in which this matter appears to us is that we want satisfaction of the understanding. If it is not proposed to give me any satisfaction in that respect—if it seems repugnant to the intention or to the judgment of other persons to satisfy me upon this matter,—pray, if my understanding is not to be at all interested, on what ground do you claim my attention, or anybody's attention, to your system, as being a reasonable system? It seems to me, if you once put it on the ground of discussion—if you once say you can get, or pride yourselves on possessing, a faith more rational than my own, it must be because you can give better reasons, explain it in a better manner, and do more to satisfy my understanding. Now, in urging this argument, I surely do no more than the gentleman on the other side proposes; and the fault may be mine in not seeing the weight of the reasons presented to us, but the fault cannot be because I require those reasons. There can be no fault in requiring the reasons, since the profession of the Christian is, that his form of faith is more rational than the form of faith of any other persons; for, if he does not make that profession, he ought to adopt the faith of other persons, and give up his own; and if he does not give up his own, it is because he deems his more rational than others. I am not wrong, therefore, in requiring that some attempt should be made to satisfy my understanding on the subject.

I see, in the province of God with respect to nature, the sort of abstract Deity of whom mention has been made in this discussion before. I see, in the province of such a Being with respect to nature, the near relation of such a Being to nature; and—if without presumption I may say it—more, the philosophic necessity of there being such a distinct and abstract entity over nature.

The existence of nature—I am now explaining, incidentally, a small part of my conception—the existence of nature all may know; it is the first act of consciousness; man tries his power upon it—he finds it boundless. When he reaches what he feels to be the confines of space, he instantly imagines something beyond in every direction. The telescope reveals what appears as limitless phenomena. Acknowledging its extent, he next comes to inquire into its age or duration—whence did this nature originate? It could not have been created—whence did it come? From nothing? That seems impossible; at least, we are unable to conceive how this miracle could have been performed.

Now, did nature come from something, as it is sometimes said? Then it was not created, but produced from pre-existing materials; then we recommence our inquiry at this point, and ask, whence came those materials? Now we can no more conceive how pre-existing materials could come from nothing, than we can conceive how the present matter could come from nothing. Then we ask, did Deity create them? But what is this new existence which we have introduced under the name of God? It cannot be matter, for then we must suppose that God and nature are one. If God, to whom we refer, and of whom we speak in this controversy, be not matter, what is it? We have no power to conceive of an existence utterly devoid of material attributes. We then refer the origin of nature to a Being, of whom it is impossible to conceive, who creates matter by a power and force which we cannot understand. Now, is this clearing up our difficulty, or is it making the confused mystery of things plainer, which is the purpose of all controversy? I think not. If any person persists in representing God as a Being—whether we understand him or not—who created all things, we have a right to ask—where was this

Being before anything existed ?   Was there a time when the God over all, was God over nothing ?   Can we believe that a God over nothing began to be out of nothing, and to create all things when there was nothing ?   Is it, therefore, not easier to believe that this stupendous and mighty frame of nature always was, and what seems to be infinite was also eternal ?   It seems to me to be so, and upon this opinion I rest; still, I explain nothing—I do not explain how matter came to be, nor do I think any man can.   Nature no man can fathom—we can only suppose, and all that is given to us is not to suppose contradiction.   Suppose we what we will, we still stand like children on the shores of eternity, who must look forward with wistful and unsatisfactory curiosity; but let the profound sense of our own littleness, which here creeps in upon us, check the dogmatic spirit, and arrest the presumptuous world—we stand in the great presence of nature, whose inspiration should be that of modesty, humility, and love.

FOURTH SPEECH.

Rev. H. TOWNLEY :—Mr. Umpire, Chairmen, ladies and gentlemen,—There is one part of Mr. Holyoake's speech, delivered at our first meeting, to which I refer with particular pleasure, for it is at once of a highly practical character, and in complete accordance with my own views. He spoke as follows :—

" I am anxious for something to come out of this issue which shall be of service to us, for we have somewhat endangered our controversy—the advantage of free speech—by not always taking care, when so many persons are inclined to protest against that privilege, not to employ it on that which is speculative, barren, beyond time, and therefore obscure ; but we should take care to employ it upon that which goes home to men's business and bosoms, and gives them something on which they can repose, and by which they shall better direct their lives."

In harmony with what has been thus so well expressed, I propose, before the debate closes, to show the important practical consequences resulting from a belief that a Deity of some kind exists.

At the same meeting, I presented a special request in the following terms :—

" There is one other quotation which I must notice. It is in page 37 :— ' If natural theologians were content to stop where they prove a superior something to exist, Atheists might be content to stop there too, and allow theologians to dream in quiet over their barren foundling.' I cannot interpret this language otherwise than as meaning, that if Deists would behave themselves properly, and not push matters too far—if they would not go ahead of reason, the Atheist would accompany them up to the point of admitting that a *superior something* does exist. I promise to be on my good behaviour, and not to push matters unreasonably far,—by no means to shoot ahead of common sense; therefore I pray our friend to declare absolutely and unhesitatingly on this platform what, in his book, he has admitted in a manner somewhat conditional and undecided."

Mr. Holyoake responded to my appeal in the following words :—

" There was a reference made to an admission of mine, that the design argument, carried out, legitimately established the existence of a limited Being. Very well; I grant that my friend was right in supposing I should be as frank in my speech as I have been in my book, and that I am willing to allow, that, so far as the design argument goes, it establishes a Being which is distinct from nature—of limited nature.''

As soon as I heard this declaration I thought, now everything, as far as this debate is concerned, which I wished for has been obtained : I may now rest from my labours ; for, as it respects this discussion, I have nothing more to seek. But, alas ! as our friend proceeded, I found that I had congratulated myself too soon, or, at least, too abundantly. There followed averments and reasonings not in harmony with my supposition.

Foremost among Mr. Holyoake's adverse reasonings stands his plea, that the design argument ends in establishing an *organized* Deity. To carry his point, he insists that in this particular argument the use of the term *person* has this effect. His views on this point are fully set forth in his "Refutation of Paley's Natural Theology," in which work he says :—

"Who was Dolland? A person, says experience. Who is God? A person, says Paley. That which can design, which can contrive, must be a person. What kind of a person was Dolland? An organized one, of course,—who ever heard of a person not organized? What kind of a person is God? An organized person, of course. An unorganized person is a carved trunk or a chiseled stone. The same experience which assures us that design had a designer, assures us that a person must be organized, because we never knew one unorganized. What kind of an organization had Dolland? Hands, and eyes, and head. Who ever heard of a man making a telescope, without a head, or hands, or eyes? What kind of an organization has Deity? Deity, the eye-maker, resembles Dolland, the telescope-maker. God made man in his own image. Deity has hands, and eyes, and head. Who ever heard of a blind God, or a Deity without a head? The vilest Hindoo imagination always puts a head on his idol."

Mr. Holyoake thus apprehends that the employment of the term "person" shows that the Deity developed by the design argument must be, like Dolland the optician, a material, organized Being. He then infers that such a Deity as this must himself manifest contrivance, and have had a maker. He further infers that this maker of the Deity must, for a similar reason, himself have been made ; and that, on the same ground, there must have been a countless series of Deities, successively deriving their existence from each other. He thus endeavours to show that the design argument leads to absurdity, and thence draws the inference that the argument itself must be unsound. In upholding his cause, at our first meeting, he employed this order of reasoning with reference to the design argument, as it was set forth by myself.

Now, I entirely dissent from our friend's opinion that the term " person " is invariably used to signify a being that is material and organized; because the word, in fact, is of *generic* import, and is used to express either an organized human being, or an *unorganized Divine Being*.

This appears from. books in common use, and to them we must repair to ascertain the *usus loquendi*,—the popular use of the particular term. The Bible is a book in popular use. I now refer to the Bible, not as to doctrine, nor as to precept, but as to a *purely literary point;* and upon such a point the Bible may bear testimony, the same as if it were a book not at all of a religious kind.

Now we find in that volume that the term " person " is employed to signify a Divine Being, *destitute of matter*, for in the commencement of the Epistle to the Hebrews we read that " Christ is the brightness of the Father's glory and the express image of his person." The apostle here is speaking, as all know who are acquainted with the New Testament, of a Being perfectly immaterial, a Being of whose essence matter forms no part. The Book of Common Prayer employs the term in the same way, both in the Litany, and in the Creed ascribed to St. Athanasius. Dr. Johnson, in his Dictionary, so uses the term, saying, in explanation of the word Trinity, that it means, " The incomprehensible union of three persons in the Godhead." There are a multitude of works of inferior popularity and note, that might be brought and put on the table by hundreds, going in the same direction. I will make one quotation from a work, entitled, " The Royal Exchange and Palace of Industry." It is from the pen of the Rev. Thomas Binney, a well-known, intelligent, and popular minister, labouring in this Metropolis. He says—

"God is not nature, nor nature God. God and the universe are not one and the same thing. He is not a force, a power, a law; he is not attraction, electricity, or any of the great active material agents, or all of them put together; he is not necessity, chance, fate; he is not a thing, nor the sum of things, but a person: he is a mind, with faculties, affections, character, and is as distinct from the earth, and the world, as a man is distinct from a house, or a clock, or anything whatever that he can call his."

By these authorities I establish my point, that the term

"person" is of *generic* import, and sometimes means an *immaterial* being.[a]

---

[a] If the word person were *not* thus generic, it would not in the slightest degree affect my argument, for *in my whole train of reasoning I never once employed it.* The term I always used was, in accordance with the wording of the question, that of *Being;* the question running thus, "Is there sufficient proof of the existence of a God; that is, of a *Being* distinct from nature?"

FIFTH SPEECH.

Mr. HOLYOAKE :—Keeping in view, as well as we are able, that the purpose of this controversy, as of all controversy, must be to make things plainer, and to reconcile what was obscure before to the understanding of persons who were not able to comprehend it in the old form of expression, I think, if we apply such a rule to the observations which we have lately heard, they will not prove quite so satisfactory as seems to the gentleman by whom we have just been favoured with them. For instance—I have no objection at all to his theory of the import of the word person in a literary sense. I know that the word person is frequently used in the sense in which my friend so used it; but my argument is, that in that sense it is not at all intelligible to us, and that in that sense I think it has nothing whatever to do with the design argument; and if that be so— if that be the sense in which it is used in reference to the design argument—then it is quite sufficient, in my view, to establish the worthlessness of that argument.[a]

For instance—he says, an organized being, of course, is a person, and a person is also an unorganized being. Now you remember that the argument our friend on the last night of debate introduced, was founded expressly and explicitly on human experience ; it was an appeal to the argument of Paley[b]—as broad an appeal as was ever made to obvious common sense[c]—to explain experimental remarks which every man makes on the appearance of nature, as a human being.

Now, therefore, he says, look over nature, and we find various things formed, which we call things designed, or contrived, or adapted ; and how came all this about ? Paley says,

---

[a] See the fourth and sixth speeches.

[b] It differed widely from Paley's argument. His was reasoning by analogy, mine by induction.

[c] It was so, because it was an inductive, not an analogical argument. *Throughout, Mr. Holyoake has, by two oversights, confounded Paley's argument by analogy with the argument by induction, and my argument by induction with the argument by analogy, and thereby rendered his reasonings irrelevant and entirely devoid of weight.* (See the sixth speech.)

that the Atheist supposes nature has power to do all this by
a mode which, indeed, we are not able to explain; but he
gives us this argument, in order that we may be able to
explain it.   He says, if you look at the matter through the
light of experience, you will be able to explain it.   We find
certain things are done; we look about, and find human
beings; various intelligences go about the world designing,
and we find in nature works analogous to their own;—we
are bound from that experience to conclude that those
works in nature also have a designer.   Then he says this
designer must be a person; but if he means a person,—if
he then passes from the experience on which he founds this
argument, to the literary sense of person, he changes altogether his ground, because if it is said the person meant is
an unorganized person, then I say you have been appealing
to my experience.   What experience have any of us of an
unorganized person ?

If I have no right to ask that question with respect to an
unorganized person,—if I have no right to appeal to experience for that,—then Paley had no right to appeal to
human experience to find out a human designer by which to
found the analogy for a Divine designer.

If it means, really, that the person to whom we have been
introduced is merely an unorganized Divine Being, or a
being without organization—a being which is contrary to
our experience—if we are to suppose that the adaptation or
contrivance of nature has been brought about in this way,
what is the difference between my supposing that nature has
done it all, and your supposing that an unorganized being
has done it all?   You can only object to my hypothesis
that I cannot explain how nature has done it.   Surely I may
object as well to your hypothesis, you cannot explain how
an unorganized Divine Being has done it.

Whatever relevancy there may be in the argument, it
turns upon the point whether we are right or not in endea-
vouring to have the matter explained.   The objection made
to the man who theorises about nature, and supposes nature
accomplishes all we see—the reason why the Christian
world rejects our explanation is, they say, you cannot explain it.   I have a right to say, when you refuse my hypothesis and give me another, that it should be explained.
If you, to convince me that some design must have had a de-

signer, refer to your human experience, I say I do not see by what right you abandon human experience, and take refuge in a literary interpretation;[d] it seems to me a new kind of argument altogether, and the first part of it is not sufficient to afford us the information of which we are in search.

I will just explain there are some terms which are frequently used in this reasoning, such as, there must be a first cause, or, there must be a power. Now, if our friend should pass from the ground of a mere Being independent of nature, to the more sublime ground which the Pantheist occupies when he talks of a first cause—a power, I should have the same difficulty in comprehending the meaning of these terms; for when we come to ask what is meant, we find out that all those things of which we have any notion are the result of combination—consist of two or more elements, out of which some new combination is produced, which we call effect; but there is no effect proceeding from a single cause—all effects proceed from two or more causes. If there was only one thing, there could be nothing else—we have no experience of any effects being produced from a single cause, so that the very language which metaphysicians and divines usually employ misleads us. The word "power" ought to be plural, because a mere single power—which has mere unity—never produces anything in human experience; every effect, every thing produced, is the result of the combination of two or more powers; we therefore ought to speak—if we speak on the ground on which Paley speaks—we ought to say, not, the first cause of all things, or, all things are produced by a great power, but we ought to speak of the first cause of all things, and the powers whereby all are produced.[e]

---

[d] I took no refuge in a literary interpretation. Mr. Holyoake had intimated that the term person (a term employed *not by me*, but by Paley,) always conveyed the idea of an organized being. I simply corrected that mistake. (See the fourth speech.)

[e] We have experience that there are effects seen in nature, the production of which requires an intelligence which common sense testifies nature does not possess. This is sufficient to establish the fact, that a Being distinct from nature—that a God—exists. (See first and eighth speeches.) Whether there be but one God, is a question not pertaining to the present debate. (See the commencement of the first speech.) When it shall have been established (and that it can be established I have no doubt) that there is but one God, then it will obviously have been also established

I have only a few moments at my disposal, and I will occupy them in what my friend was referring to. I am glad it was with a view to assure us that the solution of this question is mixed up essentially with some practical rules for our guidance, and it is important for us to know that some Being exists independent of nature, in order that we may have an adequate guide during our sojourn on earth.[f]

A person will say to me, if the Atheist is not able to believe in the existence of a Being distinct from nature, it is demanded, in what does he believe ? We answer, though he may not be able to explain the origin of all things, he may yet believe in the things themselves; though he may not be able to account for nature, it does not follow, therefore, that he disbelieves in the existence of nature.[g] Without the powers to penetrate the secret of nature, without the intuition which guesses[h] that secret, without the facts which explain it, without being convinced by any theories extant on the subject, without being able to learn of the existence of one spot of land on the wide sea of theological controversy, and amidst the tossing to and fro upon the deep of speculation, which we have no vessel adequate to navigate, nor chart nor compass to guide, from which no spiritual Columbus has ever returned, bringing a report from the New World,[i] — the Atheist, observing all this, keeps by the shore—the broad and

---

that he singly is capable of producing the supernatural effects which nature exhibits to our view. The existence of several secondary instrumental causes is not inconsistent with the existence of one sole, primary, efficient cause, by whom they are all employed and put in motion.

[f] See the tenth speech.

[g] He disbelieves the existence of that which common sense testifies to be nature, for he believes nature to contain an intelligence which common sense testifies nature does not possess. (See first and eighth speeches.)

[h] He guesses that nature possesses an intelligence adequate to the contrivance of the eye and other organs seen in nature; and, notwithstanding the protestations of common sense, believes his conjecture to be the truth and acts upon it. (See first and eighth speeches.)

[i] A skilful and well-accredited pilot exists, come from the unseen world, able and willing to navigate the frail bark of every human being, disposed to trust him, through all the shoals and storms of life; and to conduct the weakest and most undeserving of the human race safely into the haven of eternal peace and rest. (See latter part of the tenth speech.)

E

pleasant[k] shore of humanity, relinquishing the fabulous
legends which cupidity or fancy has originated, and relies on
the more useful, but less ambitious, belief of growth and
development, of science and art, of trust and truth.

---

[k] I once, at the request of a pious mother, visited a young man who
professed atheistic principles, and who was suffering from an incurable
complaint.　Misery was depicted in his countenance, and the first words
he addressed to me, when I approached his couch, were to this effect :—
" If you have come intending to do me an act of kindness, take me and
dash my brains out against this wall."　I reasoned calmly and affec-
tionately with him, and before he died he cried to the pilot referred to in
the preceding note, to come on board his perishing bark, and guide him
safely to the heavenly coast.

SIXTH SPEECH.

Rev. H. TOWNLEY:—Mr. Holyoake has further urged, that the process of *analogical reasoning*, as well as the employment of the term "person," would end in establishing a *material, organized* Deity.

On carefully perusing our friend's strictures upon Paley, and considering what he said at our first meeting, it appears to me that, unintentionally, he has committed a fundamental mistake. *The analogical mode of argumentation is grounded upon partial resemblance. In the question at issue, he has erroneously viewed it as grounded (like induction) upon total resemblance; and this error has vitiated the entire mass of his reasoning about analogy.*

That analogy is grounded upon *partial* resemblance, I will prove by three authorities. One is the "Encyclopædia Metropolitana," in which we thus read:—"Analogy, in philosophy, a species of resemblance or agreement in some respects between two or more things that *differ in other respects.*" The second is the "Encyclopædia Britannica:—"Analogy, in philosophy, a certain relation and agreement between two or more things, which in *other respects are entirely different.*" The third is our friend's work, from which I have already quoted. In his book called "A Logic of Facts," he says, "Analogy has frequently been confounded with induction. Analogy signifies reasoning from resemblances subsisting between phenomena;—induction, reasoning from the sameness of phenomena."

In accordance with the above authorities, analogy may be described as—*a process of reasoning from what is known to what is unknown, grounded upon partial resemblance.* It produces *probability;* differing from induction, which, being grounded upon *entire* resemblance, or sameness, produces *certainty.*

I did not, on the first evening of the debate, employ the argument from analogy, but that from *induction.* I will, however, this evening, throw my reasoning into the *analogical form,* to show that in that mode also it issues in establishing an *immaterial, unorganized* Divinity.   The following will now be my first proposition :—

There is an ascertained partial resemblance between organs seen in art and organs seen in nature, as, for instance, between the *telescope* and the *eye.*

There is a *resemblance* between them, there will therefore be a SIMILARITY.

In art—in the telescope, there is seen *contrivance,* for the telescope is a complicated organ or instrument formed upon mechanical and optical principles, and adapted to the purpose of vision.

In nature—in the eye, there is seen *contrivance,* for it is a complicated organ or instrument formed upon mechanical and optical principles, and adapted to the purpose of vision.

The resemblance being only *partial,* there will be DISSIMILARITY also.

In art—in the telescope, there is seen a *natural* contrivance, —a contrivance such as a natural contriver is able to produce.

In nature—in the eye, is seen a *supernatural* contrivance,— a contrivance which no natural contriver is able to produce.

The following will be my second proposition :—

It is probable, from analogy, that there is in some further respect a partial resemblance between organs seen in art and organs seen in nature—between the *telescope* and the *eye.*

It is probable that there will be in some respect a *further* SIMILARITY between them.

In art—the telescope has been produced by a *contriver:* analogy makes it probable that *in nature the eye,* also, will have been produced by a *contriver.*

Here the *further similarity* in the second proposition—*a contriver, a contriver*—reasonably answers to the similarity in the first proposition,—*a contrivance, a contrivance.*

It is probable there will be in some respect a *further* DISSIMILARITY.

In art—the telescope was produced by a *natural* contriver, who was equal to its production ; analogy makes it probable that *in nature the eye* will have been produced by a *supernatural* contriver.   Here is *dissimilarity* in the second proposition, in exact reasonable accordance with that existing in the first. *It is this dissimilarity which our friend has entirely overlooked.*

That he had not the true analogical argument in his mind
when he wrote his Refutation of Paley, is abundantly evinced
in the third chapter of his work, where he says :—

"A watch appears to be put together for a purpose—that of telling time.
Who put the watch together? Experience answers—'A man.' Our experience tells us that men have made and can make watches. Facts solve
the query. A spider appears put together for a purpose—that of catching
flies. Who put the spider together? Paley answers, 'A God.' But who
is God? What experience has made us acquainted with *this* artificer?
Theology vociferates, but facts are silent. 'It is experience which leads
us to man as the watch-maker, and it is experience which must lead us to
God as the spider-maker, before we can arrive at rational certainty about
such maker's existence."

It here appears that Mr. Holyoake had his mind occupied
about *experience*, which leads to *certainty*, and not about
analogy, of which *probability* is the result; and that the
real analogical process of reasoning he had not in view.
Thus the plea grounded upon *analogy* fails him, as did
that built upon the term person. His two pillars are removed from under him; his argument falls to the ground;
but mine remains unmoved.

Further, Mr. Holyoake, in that part of his first speech to
which I have referred, alluding to my argument, as I originally set it forth, did not hesitate honestly to admit that it
went to establish *a Being distinct from nature,*[a] and *such a
Being* is of necessity *immaterial.*[b]

---

[a] See pages 21 and 43, and Appendix B.

[b] Thus it appears that my argument, whether constructed analogically,
as on the second evening, or inductionally, as on the first, establishes an
immaterial, unorganized Deity of some kind, and thereby *substantiates
all for which in the present discussion it was needful for me to contend.*

SEVENTH SPEECH.

Mr. Holyoake :—I believe, if you regard what my friend is saying, it will be impossible to deny but that this discussion will have a very satisfactory termination, for his satisfaction seems to be very great. However, it will conduce more to your instruction to notice, not so much about what we say as to each other's feelings, as about each other's argument.

When I was opening this discussion, some persons manifested dislike to my desiring something like a rational explanation upon this subject, and also upon my explaining that I thought we inquired to no purpose, unless we came to some deliberate, to some distinct, to some conclusive opinion upon the matter about which we are debating. But my friend has so warned me against expecting certainty, thinking it is a great mistake on my part to be looking in this argument for certainty, that I am disposed to think he is of opinion that certainty is not what I ought to expect. Now, if I ought not to expect certainty on his side, surely I may be excused for resting in uncertainty on my own.[a]

What he has said about my admission—that the design argument proves, as far as it goes, the existence of something—is proper enough; but why I say that that something will be barren is, that it does not prove that which we set out to seek. I say that something exists, and that is all I have said—*that* the design argument appears to lead us to, and leaves it an open question whether that something shall be a Being independent of nature, or nature itself.[b]

I presume, since our controversy is—since what our friend undertakes to establish is—the affirmative of the proposition —not merely that something exists, but something independent of nature exists—you see now he is desirous for me to

---

[a] *Probability* producing *belief*, not demonstration producing certainty, is that which the question in debate calls for.

[b] It has been both proved by myself and admitted by Mr. Holyoake, virtually in his Paley's Natural Theology Refuted, and explicitly in this debate, that my argument goes to establish the existence of a Being distinct from nature. (See pages 21 and 42).

concede something exists, yet it is not that he wants to prove; my concession that something exists amounts only to this—it only opens the field to further discussion. What is the something? My answer is—nature is that something, which is superior to man both in power, and in art, and in all contrivances displayed.[c]

He has argued that something exists independent of nature—he has done no more; and the old process to which he has been explaining, with so much instruction to myself, and with profit to all, of the nature of all analogy, only shows me, more conclusively than I saw it before, how very unsatisfactory is the ground on which he is reposing even his own argument. He tells us that analogy signifies partial resemblance, not total similarity. Of course, I am well aware of that. The extract he read is a proof that I was aware of it; the fact that I have been arguing in contradiction to the maxim is a proof that I have been aware of it from the beginning; but I say, if that is all you mean by your argument, that it is merely a matter of analogy—if it is only a matter of partial resemblance, I say you can get from it no complete proof—that if you merely found it upon partial resemblance, there is no demonstration there whatever, and your cause is no better, no sounder than I have before described it[d]—as being merely your conjecture about a Being independent of nature; it is merely a conjecture, merely a suggestion, just like my own conjecture[e]—like my own suggestion about nature being that one great Being about which we are all concerned.

He states, the ground on which his argument reposes may in some respects be agreement, and in some respects contradiction, but all analogies in that manner are open to likeness and to dissimilarity; that is perfectly true, and why I wish that to be pointed out is, to show you that what we came into

---

[c] To sustain this allegation there is nothing but conjecture; against it there is the testimony of common sense. (See the first and eighth speeches.)

[d] *Probability*, arising from a preponderance of proof and argument, is what the terms of the question calls for. To *certainty*, arising from demonstration, the question does not refer.

[e] There is a wide gulf between *probability*, arising from a preponderance of proof and argument grounded on common sense, and *conjecture*, for which common sense gives no warrant. (See the eighth speech.)

this controversy for, is to get certainty;[f] and my purpose is to explain, what my friend has been explaining, that the ground on which he reposes for certainty,[g] is simply the partial ground of analogy, which can do no more than suggest —which cannot demonstrate, cannot give us the certainty we seek.

Now, if you say you suggest, you merely suggest the existence of a Being independent of nature; if all you do is to suggest, then I am on the same ground as yourself, when I come to you and make a suggestion about nature. There is that theory of suggestion which the Pantheist puts on that ground alone, and, if we may follow suggestion, I submit the suggestion of Pantheism is more practical, is more interesting, and is far more probable, than the suggestion founded on the design argument, as founded by Paley, and as repeated in this discussion, because it is far more natural to say that nature is God, because nature is the source to us of every marvel and every blessing we enjoy in life; and we know also, in following the same course, that nature is propitiated, as it were, by science, and not propitiated by any other means whatever.

I might say—following the same course of suggestion— that the stars do sing as they shine, and that we will hear the music of the spheres, not merely in poetry, but in fact; that everything does speak in an audible voice; that in the ringing of the bell we will hear the exclamation of matter on being struck; in the rumbling of the earth, as the waggon moves along, we will acknowledge the groaning under oppression; the roaring of the waters, as they rise from their beds,

---

[f] The terms of the question, among which terms demonstration and certainty have no place, show that to obtain *certainty* was *not* the design of the present controversy; but to obtain *probability* sufficient for practical purposes.

[g] I have at no time in this debate declared that certainty is that which I intended to establish. My argument, thrown into the analogical form on the second evening for the purpose of showing how Mr. Holyoake had misapprehended the true process of reasoning by analogy, proves probability only. My original argument (see page 6) is in the inductive form, and not having been overthrown, goes to establish certainty; but I claimed probability merely, as its effect, probability being all that it was incumbent upon me to prove; and, by proving this, atheism would receive its death-blow, for *the difference between the probable existence of a God of some kind and the probable non-existence of a God of any kind, is the substantial and fundamental difference between theism and atheism.*

shall be the expression of their throes, as they continue to
be convulsed; the thunder-peal shall be only the sublime
protest of electricity against being dragged from its car, and
the flashing of the lightning shall be but the evidence of the
last indignation of the offended elements; and, descending to
the ever beautiful world again, we may exclaim, as Words-
worth does in his apostrophe to the daisy,

> " So fair, so sweet, withal so sensitive ;—
> Would that the little flowers were born to live
> Conscious of half the pleasure which they give :—
> That to this mountain-daisy's self were known
> The beauty of its star-shaped shadow, thrown
> On the smooth surface of this naked stone."

Why, I say, if you will follow the theory merely of suggestion, there are no suggestions of more fascination, no
suggestions more sublime, or better founded, than the suggestions of pantheism. Surely, the disparity which has
hitherto been supposed to exist between the two systems is
not diminished by the design argument of Paley, or any
argument you can produce. The moment you show it is
merely one of analogy, I say we have a right to bring in our
analogy, and to make our suggestion by the side of yours.

But I will show concisely that the great point at issue
is, not that we should make these things probable, because
there were probabilities understood amongst us before,—
we hold our controversy for a far more important and solemn
purpose; we hold it to come to some conclusion—that we
should have certainty about it. I want not merely to be
under the impression that partial analogy will suggest—I
want to know whether it is so, or whether it can be proved
or not—I want to know whether we have power, by unaided
reason, to say with certainty we know a Being exists independent of nature, who shall become the object of homage,
admiration, and praise.

That is the essential point of the controversy; because, if
that can be proved, and we fail to find it out, then there is
an imputation upon our intelligence, or a more serious imputation upon our want of industry, or want of belief, upon
those points upon which you are not able to arrive at certainty.

You see, therefore, the whole of this controversy turns on
the point of what degree of certainty can by any possibility be

established.   I will say, my own impression is, the only conclusions to which we can come, are those which are expressed in those lines of CARLILE, which were quoted in the *Times* newspaper,—a very unusual place to find them, but which seem to sum up all that can be established by mere reason in these controversies :—

"Divines can say—"

on the other side of the question, with respect to the Deity,—

"Divines can say but what themselves believe ;
Strong proofs they have, but not demonstrative ;
For were all sure, then all minds would agree,
And faith itself be lost in certainty.
To live uprightly,[h] then, is sure the best ;
To save ourselves, and not to damn the rest."

---

[h] A genuine faith is a great help to a good life, and *a genuine faith results from real evidence producing probability*. In order to live uprightly, therefore, probability is of great importance :—and a view of probability as valueless, neither springs from reason, nor leads to righteousness.

EIGHTH SPEECH.

Rev. H. Townley :—I remember an anecdote related by the Rev. John Newton, respecting the whale-fishery. "There are skilful and daring men," he said, "who go out upon that perilous service. They harpoon the monster of the deep, and then they throw out a few black kegs, as a decoy. The whale lashes these black kegs with its tail, and in the meantime its harpooners effect their escape." I do not mean to go after any black kegs that our friend may have thrown out as a decoy, but to keep to my main argument.

Our friend, in order to maintain his opinion that nature is adequate to the production of all we see, appears to me to have allowed his reasoning faculty to turn a deaf ear to common sense. I say it with all respect, but my argument requires it to be said. He has allowed his reasoning faculty to turn a deaf ear, in this particular instance, to common sense, and to hearken to *conjecture* in its stead.

Reason is the supreme judge in the human mind, but, like other judges, it may discharge its functions properly or improperly. A judge acts properly when his decisions are influenced by intelligent and competent witnesses; improperly, when he is affected by witnesses of an opposite character.

There are two witnesses which are continually presenting themselves at the bar of reason. One of them is *common sense*—a witness of the right stamp, intelligent and competent, for common sense testifies respecting things which it has *seen*, and which it *knows to exist*. The other is *conjecture*, unintelligent and incompetent, testifying to things it has not seen, and does not know to exist. Our friend has, I fear, in this particular instance, allowed his reason to be influenced in its decisions by *conjecture*, rather than by the opposite witness.

Common sense has perceived no power, and knows no power in nature adequate to the production of the contrivances which nature exhibits; and reports to reason that no such power exists : conjecture testifies that nature has such power.

If our friend had required his reason to hearken to the

testimony of common sense, instead of conjecture, his reason would have declared that the contrivances seen in nature are beyond the power of nature to produce; and that such contrivances can be accounted for only upon the hypothesis that there is a supernatural contriver who produced them.

I am quite aware that reasoning may at times, and especially in the infancy of the human race, draw erroneous conclusions from the reports made by common sense. Witness, in bygone days, the declaration that the sun went round the earth, grounded on the report of common sense, that the sun appeared to rise in the east, and to set in the west. But it by no means follows from this, that the testimony of conjecture is to be preferred to that of common sense. It was not conjecture that enabled reason to correct its error respecting the revolution of the sun, but common sense. Common sense reported to reason a multitude of additional astronomical phenomena which it had seen, both with and without telescopic aid; and it was because reason was influenced by the enlarged testimony of common sense, and not at all because it hearkened to conjecture, that reason in this matter pronounced a different decision.

Now, had it been only in the infancy of mankind that common sense had reported to reason that there were organisms and contrivances in nature, to produce which there appeared no sufficient amount of intelligence in nature, but that, as time rolled on, as microscopic aid began to be afforded, as matter began to be examined with greater care and attention, common sense had discovered and reported to reason, that at length intelligence was found in matter adequate to the production of all the contrivances that nature exhibits—had this been the case, I would have been as forward as our friend in preferring the later reports of common sense to those of an earlier time, and in requiring reason to hearken to them, and to reverse the decision it had originally pronounced.

But such has not been the case. Microscopes (some of them magnifying half a million of times) have been invented, and employed in the frequent examination of particles of matter, by the most scientific men, with the greatest care and attention; but common sense is as far as ever from discovering any appearance of intelligence in them whatsoever.

Will our friend declare that we have not waited long enough to ascertain what there is in nature—that, though the required intelligence is not *now* displayed to common sense by nature, it is expected that it will be *at some future time;* and that, till such time arrives, nature ought to have credit for being now in the possession of such intelligence; and thus, there being no need for the agency of a supernatural being, we should believe that no such supernatural being exists?

Ought our friend to make such a declaration as this? Would it not imply that he had rather his reason should hearken to the testimony of conjecture than to that of common sense? Will our friend permit Archdeacon Paley to allow his reason to act in this manner? He gives no such license. In Mr. Holyoake's work on Paley, we read,

"Speaking of the mind of the Deity, Paley says, 'Every animated being has its sensorium. This sphere *may* be enlarged to an indefinite extent; *may* comprehend the universe; and being so imagined, *may* serve to furnish us with as good a notion of God, as we are capable of forming of the immensity of the Divine nature.'"

Mr. Holyoake then puts a pointed, and, in my judgment, a proper question,—" Why is everything to be left to *may bees*, and to imagination?" And I may ask the question, " Why does our friend himself take a license which he refuses to Archdeacon Paley?"

Will he say that as particles of matter are reported by common sense to be possessed of *self-moving* power, this power is enough to account for the formation of the eye and other human organs? Without stopping to debate whether common sense, after the innumerable observations it has made, will not, on the contrary, affirm that, in order to self-motion, there must be life—without stopping to debate this, let it, for argument's sake, be granted, that a particle of matter can move itself. I then ask, can it *guide itself* also? An eye is to be formed; some millions of corpuscles, or particles of matter, are required, in order to its formation—if each of these millions of particles has power to move itself, is it able also *to guide* itself into its own proper position in the forthcoming organ? Has it intelligence enough to do this? And if it has, I yet further ask, would even such intelligence as this meet the exigency of the case? *Intelligence is wanted sufficient to have contrived the eye.* Unless such intelligence as this be possessed, the requirements of the case are not met; reason is not satisfied; *reason requires an adequate contriver;* if one cannot be found in nature, it must be sought for out of nature—have one, reason must, and reason will.

If there were in a field a vast multitude of self-moving, self-guiding bricks, and beams, and stones, and, in order to form an intended edifice, each of these building materials had power and intelligence to move itself into its own proper place in the roof, or in the floor, or in the wall; still, the final appearance of a commodious and well-contrived habitation cannot be accounted for but upon the hypothesis that *some architect, possessed of adequate intelligence, had made the plan.* The self-moving, self-guiding materials would no more account for the edifice than the labourers, who with their hands moved and guided into their appropriate places the bricks, beams, and stones of which St. Paul's cathedral is composed, would account for the erection of that noble structure. A Sir Christopher Wren must be found. For the erection of the yet more noble temple of the human body, a greater than Sir Christopher Wren is wanted. To accomplish this *there must be a God.*

NINTH SPEECH.

Mr. Holyoake :—With regard to the amusing story of the capture of the whale and the black kegs, I think our friend will hardly do me the injustice of saying, that all the arguments I have submitted to his notice have been of that nature. I think there were one or two things which went very much to the root of the matter, and which deserved a somewhat different designation than that of being merely black kegs. I think, when I pointed out to him that if he asserted that the word person, in the sense in which he used it in the design argument, meant an unorganized Being, that that phrase explained nothing, and that I have just as much right to say that nature, to which he has been referring, produces all the marvels which we observe by its own power, not being able to explain how it is done, it is just as reasonable for me to ascribe it to nature, without giving explanation, as to say it was done by some unorganized Being, of which I can also give no explanation whatever.

Again, I reminded him that his own explanation, upon the ground on which his argument reposed, was, that it was essentially partial in its nature, that it amounted to a suggestion, that it did not amount to demonstration at all,—merely made his side of the question probable. I submitted that that was by no means sufficient for the purpose which we had in view. In the argument he did not notice it,[a]—he has not explained the sense in which he would regard it, or how it should stand in our understandings.[b]

There was also the concession which he so wished, namely, that something should be allowed to exist. Unless he shall be able to connect that something with a Being independent of nature, with a Being independent of all the attributes of nature, which he proposes to establish,—without he shows that that concession involved that, I do not see how his side of the controversy is substantially advanced.

Thus far for the main points, so far as I have been able to elucidate them, which came out of this controversy, looking exclusively at the line of argument he adopted.

---

[a] See note g, page 56.   [b] See pages 21 and 43.

I shall introduce some other reflections, besides those he has introduced, but I do so because the matter which he himself has presented does not seem sufficient to occupy the time at my disposal; and because, if I stood here merely on the negative ground, to criticise what he might bring forward, the controversy would pass away, and you would know nothing of my notions. I have as much right to interlocute some of my notions as my friend has to explain his. What I advanced may come under the denomination of black kegs, but it absolutely relates, much more closely than that phrase would imply, to what it is proper for you to consider and for me to introduce.

I am particularly concerned, as I have been throughout, to explain, with all the explicitness I am able, that if I take up with any other hypothesis, it must be because I am able to understand it. If I adopt a theory of nature which I cannot explain to others, why, plainly, I am dumb when I go before them. I will tell my friend more than that:—that if any man can put into my hand an argument in favour of the existence of Deity, which I can go with to the public and defy their judgment, which is my custom with the arguments I adduce, then I will go and develop that with as much pride and pleasure as I now develop those views which I entertain.

All I require is, that some man will arm us, that I may dare other people. I cannot submit to go and supplicate[c] people to think on my side of the case. I only care for that

---

[c] Man cannot help believing, when he duly investigates and ponders real evidence. But he has the power (alas, too often exercised!) of altogether turning away from evidence which goes to establish a result strongly opposed to his inclination; or, which amounts in effect to the same thing, of considering solid evidence, not for the purpose of estimating its weight, but that of neutralizing it by ingenious but hollow argument. I find many of my fellow-men, as I once was myself, averse to religion, and consequently indisposed to give careful and candid attention to proofs and arguments tending to prove the necessity of a religious life. Unless I can counterwork this indisposition, my ultimate practical design will not be accomplished. I think that I am likely to prevail by presenting my arguments in the language of *entreaty* rather than in that of *defiance*. I therefore entreat those with whom I argue—not to believe without evidence—but candidly to investigate and ponder the evidence, that they may believe. In such a case as this, where the best interests of my fellow-men are at stake, "to beg I am" *not* "ashamed."

statement which I feel no man can disqualify, no man can explain away. If I cannot feel the defiance on my presenting it, then I cannot present it; but whoever should give to me one reasonable argument, I should go and proclaim it as readily as any I now entertain.

When my friend talks so much about matter, and about what it cannot do, and tells us that the telescope has revealed many marvels, as indeed it has, and many marvels utterly irreconcilable with the popular theology of the day, but in the direction we are now speaking,—and has made it more and more impossible to conceive, in the development of nature and its wondrous manifestations, more and more impossible to conceive that nature is not capable of doing all those things itself, he must assume—he does not say it—but his reasoning proceeds upon this very great hypothesis, namely, that he knows all that matter can do, and all that it cannot do.[d] If he does not know that, I wonder by what right he says so plainly that the wonders he observes in nature are not the work of nature, but of some Being above nature.

That which repels me from that aspect of the argument is its amazing presumption[e]—the amount of knowledge it implies. I am willing, indeed, to wait for more of the process of years to explain, if need be, the miracles and marvels of nature; but when I see wonders like those which nature perpetually presents in its inorganic manifestations, as well as its vegetable and organic manifestations—not to go elsewhere,—when, I say, I discover a curious construction in a tree far transcending anything which human intelligence can construct, I am disposed to ascribe that to the work of nature. The only objection that my friend makes is, not that he knows nature cannot do that, for he knows nothing

---

[d] Universal common sense does most distinctly testify that matter has exhibited no signs whatever of possessing the intelligence necessary to contrive the human eye and countless multitudes of such-like organs. All that atheism can do is to *conjecture* that, nevertheless, such intelligence is possessed by nature. But thus to *turn a deaf ear to common sense, and to exercise faith upon the report which mere conjecture makes, is to act in opposition to the dictates of sound philosophy.* (See first and eighth speeches.)

[e] To reject the testimony which is furnished by common sense, and to accept that which is furnished by conjecture, indicates presumption; for it is to separate reason from its appointed handmaid, common sense, and to yoke it with the false guide, conjecture.

F

of the kind,—all he can object to is, that I cannot explain it,* then he has no right to put down my hypothesis because I cannot explain it, unless he can put in place of mine a better, which he can explain.

Plainly, I rest my argument there. It is not with me a matter of account. I make no pretence to account for everything. I do not pretend to account for what I find in nature. I do not feel called upon to account for it. I do not know that I am required to account for it; but I say, if any man will demand of me to account for the manifestations of nature—if we must leave off to study the manner of nature and the process of nature, and to predicate about the order of nature—if, I say, we must come to that,—an occupation, a proud one, an intellectually luxurious one, to which I am not averse,—I say, if we come to that, none of us can have any pretence to occupy public attention unless we can explain something; and I submit, upon that ground, if you adopt my hypothesis of nature doing those things, you must except the other hypothesis, that they are done by something superior to nature. But we have no necessity to multiply the invention of processes by which we think we can account for everything. If they do not explain phenomena, I would rather express my ignorance of phenomena, my desire to find them out, my desire to have them explained; but at the same time my disinclination to pretend, by the invention of a Being above nature, to explain those miracles which plainly transcend my comprehension.

The refuge which one might take in a *may be*, my friend very properly said we ought not to put up with. To say, it *may be*, is very true, and there is nothing hardly you can suppose in favour of which you may not say it may be; but the result, the purpose of all inquiry is, not to ascertain what may be, but, if possible, to determine what is. I remember hearing a friend say, in a controversy like this, what was meant by design was that faculty in which something was done in nature which could not be done by any human being except by the exercise of intelligence— except by the exercise of a cultivated intelligence. I re-

---

* My objection is, that matter *shows no signs* of possessing such intelligence as is necessary to contrive the wondrous organisms visible in the vegetable and animal kingdoms.

member reminding him of one illustration of a thing done by a gentleman. I remember once seeing, in the Mechanic's Institution, a lecturer take a plate of glass, and suspend it between two corks, taking some sea sand, drawing a bow upon the side, and the result was, the sand on the surface disposed itself in the geometrical form of a Dutch garden. Now, being a student of geometry at the time, it occurred to me to try the case. I could not, but by the exercise of much ingenuity, by the exercise of some weeks of study, learn how to produce geometrically this sort of figure, which I saw produced by purely mechanical means. I should have been justified in saying there was intelligence, there was design, either in the glass or the sand, or the instrument whereby this wondrous effect was produced;[g] and there are many cases in nature which perpetually occur, which are evidence of design, transcending anything we are able to do—equal always to anything we can do ; just the same sort of manifestations as we produce by the exercise of our own intelligence ; and the same sort of argument would oblige us to say the same sort of intelligence resided in inorganic and inert matter.

I think the whole of these arguments go to discredit matter, to make it a second-hand tool,[h] instead of regarding it as being possessed of a power to do what it has done, until we are sure, having sifted it all through, that it is unable to perform that which we ascribe to it.

The ground on which I have attached more importance than I otherwise should to a principle which hitherto has not been very much recognised,—I mean that in this case,—is, the understanding, if possible, should be addressed. People have sometimes compared theology to a French dinner, of which you do not know the ingredients, nor the manner whereby they are compounded. I remember, in an Essay by

---

[g] There was no more proof of a designing intelligence in the glass or in the sand, or in the instrument referred to, than there is proof of a designing intelligence in the spring, or in the chain, or in the wheels of a watch, which make the hands on the dial move round in an orderly way. (See first and eighth speeches.)

[h] The atheistic line of argument goes to exalt particles of matter above the human mind, by representing them as the maker of the human mind ; the result of which, if true, would be, that as a maker rules the thing which it makes, so particles of matter would rule the human mind. Such a result is not witnessed ; and from such result reason revolts.

M. Guizot, it is said of some Eastern worshippers, that on going into the temple they were accustomed to leave their shoes at the door. He said, at some modern temples they leave their understandings at the door, and it is very well for them if they find them when they come out again.[i]

I am concerned to say, as plainly as I can, that it seems to me that the whole of this argument turns upon the question, how far we can satisfy our understandings about the phenomena of nature. A man will come to me and say, Can you account for this? Can you account for that? Now, he expects me to tell him all about everything, just as though I was present at the beginning of nature, and knew all its manifestations. If I cannot do it, he will not admit my plea of ignorance[k]—he will not admit the propriety of my saying, I do not know. Probably he smiles at my want of capacity, or my obstinate ignorance of this matter. I say to this person, Give us your own explanation—if you can make that plain which was not plain to me before, you make me your debtor, and you contribute to the public interest. All I say is, let the public judge between us, and see whether or not, in the way of explaining to the understanding, those gentlemen come any nearer to the case than we do.

I must trouble you for a moment with the aspect of nature as it appears to me, from the point of sight in which I am accustomed to regard it, because I am concerned to show it is not what is called speculatism, or atheism—to use a theological term which does not apply to it—it is not atheism, that makes the world without God. The argument sometimes employed against us is, we take God away from the world. We find the world without God, in the way we explain it. Science has shown us we are under the dominion of general laws, and that there is no special Providence, and that prayers are useless, and that propitiation is vain; that whether there be a Deity independent of nature, or whether

---

[i] As long as reason holds close fellowship with *common sense*, there is no danger of its being unhinged. Reason is in peril when it makes *conjecture* its bosom friend. (See the eighth speech.)

[k] It is Mr. Holyoake's virtual plea of *knowledge* to which I object. He pleads that nature possesses superhuman intelligence, as if he knew that it did; whereas that it possesses so glorious an attribute *he has no evidence whatever.* *He is waiting for such evidence,*—a clear proof that he does not possess it.

nature be God, it is still the God of the iron foot, that passes on without heeding,[1] without feeling, and without resting,—that nature[m] acts with a fearful uniformity, stern as fate, absolute as tyranny, merciless as death; too vast to praise, too inexplicable to worship, too inexorable to propitiate; it has no ear for prayer, no heart for sympathy, no arm to save. We reap from it neither special help nor special knowledge; it protects itself from our curiosity by giving us only finite powers; its silence is profound, and when we ask its secret, it points to death. Yet, if we are wise to learn from this great mystery, before which creeds are shattered and dogmas are cancelled, it is a magnificent monitor. Men fable to us the future with fearful presumption,—they dazzle us with a world they have never visited, amaze us with images they have never seen, alarm us by the ideal and cheat us of the real, and betray us, by a false dependence, to our own destruction.

But nature refers us to science for help, and to humanity for sympathy; love to the lovely is our only homage, study our only praise, quiet submission to the inevitable our duty, and work is our only worship.[n]

I allude to these considerations because I am not more disposed to pass from the discussion than I was to enter into it, without saying that the mere barrenness of it, as to this point—as to whether there exists a Being independent of nature—is to me unsatisfactory, it would not interest me, would not be an apology for my appearance and the occupation of your time. I do think we occupy too much of public attention by mere discussions and reiterations of opinion upon those abstract points which have no relation to human destiny or progress. The great practical question is, whether

---

[1] This statement is utterly at variance with fact. (See the latter part of the tenth speech.)

[m] Nature without a God does, indeed, answer to the terrific description of it which Mr. Holyoake here gives; and, such being the case, how comes it to pass that Mr. Holyoake is so charmed and fascinated by nature, as at times to pronounce a eulogium upon it which none but a perfect Deity deserves? (See quotation from Mr. Holyoake's "Logic of Death," given in the first speech, pp. 8, 9.)

[n] To make the description complete, it should be added, "and having no hope in God, *gloom is our constant companion.*" (See the latter part of the tenth speech.)

there exists a Deity to whom we can appeal, who is the Father of his children, and who is to be propitiated by prayer, and who will render us help in the hour of danger and distress ?

That is the great practical question. If any man can make known a Deity of that kind, he is the benefactor of all of us, —we will listen with greedy ear to all he can say. But if our experience tells us this is not the case—if we see men living and perishing year by year, not taking due care of the monitions which might affect their lives—I say, however generous the theory of those gentlemen, however well-disposed, or howmuchsoever of mercy they may proclaim to us, it amounts to no more than this—whatever may be their intentions, if this help comes not, if this Being is not to be propitiated, those who believe in it are betrayed to material destruction.

As this is the last speech I have to deliver, it becomes me to express my acknowledgments to Mr. Townley for the manner in which he has conducted his part of the discussion, speaking, as he did, with the prejudices of the public in his favour—speaking, as he has the advantage of doing, more in accordance with the education of the majority of the persons here, and with their sympathies, than I have done. It is always possible for disorder to be created by appeals to passion, or by the introduction of phrases which disturb the public.

Now, in the utter absence of all those phrases and appeals by Mr. Townley, he has done more to preserve order than I could do ; and I am concerned to thank him for this, because I attach much importance to these opportunities of controversy on this question; and if there was a noise, the people outside would appeal against the privilege, and would bring discussion into contempt. I therefore thank you on my own part, and I hope you will hear whatever my friend has to say, with the same placidness and order with which you have heard all that has hitherto passed.

TENTH SPEECH.

Rev. H. Townley :—I beg to offer an apology for having employed the illustration of " the kegs," and to say, if I have hurt our friend's feelings, by relating the anecdote about the whale, I sincerely regret it.

There are many points to which I should have referred, had time allowed; but I must now redeem my pledge, and point out the important practical results of believing that a Deity of some kind exists.

From such a belief forthwith springs up the great primary moral question, *In what relation do we stand to such a Being?* The answer must certainly be, in that of *filial;* he is our Father, we are his offspring; for the same processes of research and reasoning which make us acquainted with the existence of a God, make us also acquainted with the fact, that this God is, in the highest sense, our Maker, our *Father.*

A great practical question next arises,—*What duties devolve upon us, in consequence of the filial relation in which we stand to God?* Reason, I submit, suggests to us some of the following duties, pertaining both to our minds and inward feelings, and to our lives and outward conduct.

We ought, as his children, to have a strong desire *to hold intercourse with him;* we ought to *desire* such intercourse, with the view of becoming better acquainted with his attributes and actions,—of enjoying the happiness arising from communion with him,—of obtaining instruction from him as to the particular way in which we ought to act toward him, toward our neighbour, and toward ourselves; and as to what awaits us after death. With the view of receiving succour and comfort from him,—of obtaining his smile of approval if we have acted properly, and his forgiveness of any thing we have done amiss.

Such intercourse we ought diligently to *seek,* by instituting the inquiry, whether God has made any verbal communication of himself to mankind, respecting the possibility and method of holding fellowship with him? Reason cannot, I think, but deem it exceedingly desirable that such a communication should be possessed; for it must be admitted, that nature sheds but a very feeble light upon the pathway that leads us back to God.

Such an inquiry ought to be carried on by examining with candour and diligence such documents as have any appearance, though it should seem but plausible, of containing a communication from God; by conversing, as we have opportunity, with those of our fellow-men who have earnestly desired and endeavoured to obtain intercourse with him; by offering up prayer to him, that he would assist us in our endeavours, as we assist our children in theirs.

Reason, as soon as the existence of a God of any kind sustaining a parental relation to us is rendered probable, calls for a course of action, substantially in accordance with that which I have now pointed out.

I must here notice another part of our friend's first address, which is of a very solemn and impressive kind, and worthy of being pondered, especially in connexion with the practical observations I have just made, for it tends much to enforce attention to them. "When we pass through the inexorable gates of the future," Mr. Holyoake said, at our first meeting; "when we pass through that vestibule where Death stands opening his everlasting gates as widely to the pauper as to the king; when we pass out here, into the dim mysteries of the future, to confront, it may be, the interrogatories of the Eternal—I apprehend, every man's responsibility will go with him, and no second-hand opinions will answer for us. Nothing can justify us, nothing can give us confidence, but the conscientious nature of our own conclusions; nothing can give us courage but innocence; nothing can serve our turn but having believed according to the best of our judgment, and having followed those principles which seem to us to be the truth."

Were it not that I believe that *I have found* a revelation from God my Father, telling me how I may gain access to his footstool; were it not that I know, that by acting in accordance with what I apprehend to be such revelation, I have been rendered *an exceedingly better and happier man than I ever was before;* were it not that I further know, that I have had just the kind of heavenly feeling which I should expect to have, on the supposition that I had really held intercourse with God;—were it not for these things, what you have just listened to, as uttered by our friend, would be enough to inspire me with alarm.

Observe, particularly, he said, that after death, should there prove to be a God, *nothing could give us courage when about to appear before him but our innocence.* Is our friend himself, I would ask, like the drifted snow, entirely spotless? Is he perfectly innocent? If he is, I am not.[*]

I want to be assured that my faults and follies are all forgiven, and will not accompany me into the eternal world. The assurance that they are forgiven, I enjoy, and with it a peace that passeth all understanding. I look not at futurity with the eyes of Mr. Holyoake. He says, in "The Logic of Death :"—

"What went before and what will follow me I regard as two black impenetrable curtains, which hang down at the two extremities of human life, and which no living man has yet drawn aside. Many hundreds of generations have already stood before them, with their torches, guessing anxiously what lies behind. On the curtain of futurity many see their own shadows, the forms of their own passions, enlarged and put in motion; they shrink in terror at this image of themselves.

"A deep silence reigns behind this curtain; no one once within will answer those he has left without; all you can hear is a hollow echo of your question, as if you shouted into a chasm."

Death to him appears as a *large black impenetrable curtain*—certainly a gloomy object. It does not so appear to me. To me it is a bright transparency. To me it especially so appeared, in two very trying events. One, when I was asleep at midnight, in a sinking boat, on the wide Ganges. I was suddenly awoke, and a watery grave presented itself to my view. I thought how abrupt will be my departure from time into eternity!—how unexpected this!— in less than a short hour I shall be in the unseen world! A favourite hymn rushed into my thoughts, and was expressive of the feeling of unspeakable happiness which I experienced. The hymn thus begins :—

---

[*] And, alas! I do not stand alone in this respect. The writer of one of the articles in *The Reasoner* (No. 314, p. 458) says, "Who am I, with this load of sins upon my back, that I dare cast a stone even at the most degraded of my fellow-creatures?" Can one conscious of so much guilt plead *innocent,* before the Eternal; and if not, what is to be his fate?

"There is a land of pure delight,
  Where saints immortal reign;
Infinite day excludes the night,
  And pleasures banish pain.
"Sweet fields, beyond the swelling flood,
  Stand dressed in living green;
So to the Jews old Canaan stood,
  While Jordan rolled between."

The other instance was in the neighbourhood of Calcutta, when seized with the cholera. My life hung in suspense, and I knew that in about ten minutes it would be decided whether I was for this world, or for that still future. I then, in substance, said to those around me, that which was the language of my heart:—"I have neither fear nor sorrow. It is a lottery, but there are only prizes in the wheel. If I live, I shall have the happiness of serving my Divine Master yet longer upon earth. If I die, I shall go to him, and be for ever in his blissful presence."

I know, as our friend does, what it is to see death as a sable curtain. I have, in substance, experienced formerly what is his experience now. I have travelled the road of unbelief, and know its dismal scenery, and the gloomy goal to which it leads. When a young man, I read Hume's Essays; I associated with infidels, I imbibed their sentiments, and neglected all religious observances of every kind. My worldly calling was respectable and lucrative, and I bore a fair character among my kindred, my clients, and my neighbours. All things outwardly were prosperous and smiling, when suddenly the symptoms of a wasting disorder, which I thought in about three months would end my life, appeared. Death did then indeed appear to me as an unwelcome visitor clothed in crape. My conscience told me that I had not acted ingenuously with a book professing to be the Word of God; that I had not given it that thorough and candid investigation which it deserved. I resolved to spend the remnant of my days in the earnest pursuit of truth. I determined that if that book, upon due examination, should answer to its appellation, I would act in harmony with its dictates; if otherwise, I would lay it aside and meet death without it in the best way I could.

I read, and pondered what I read. I searched, and made inquiry. My health soon returned; but I continued my investigation of the Scriptures, I think I may say, without a day's intermission, for a year. The result was, that all my doubts and objections were cleared away, and I became a believer. I began then, I trust, in real earnest, to try to please my Maker and my Saviour, and to make my fellow-creatures happy; and from that time to this, a period of above forty years, I have lived a conscientious life, waking in the morning, and lying down at night, with a peaceful breast, and a hope full of immortality.

Would that Mr. Holyoake saw death with my eyes! That is my heart's desire. I long to see his black impenetrable drapery turned into my brilliant transparency; and what I desire for him, I desire for every one here present—I desire for every human being throughout the world. My sincerity in this desire has been proved, for I have travelled thirty thousand miles for the good of others; fifteen thousand to Calcutta (where I laboured to promote the happiness of my fellow-men, at my own cost, for several years), and fifteen thousand back to my native land. Pardon the egotism for the motive's sake.

I have now, in conclusion, to thank you all, for the attention which you have paid to my argument,—to thank you, Mr. Umpire, and the Chairmen, for the impartial and able manner in which you have discharged your duties; and you, Mr. Holyoake, for the courteous way in which you have conducted your part of the debate ; and my heart's desire and prayer is (for I do pray, and I always find, and have found for the last forty years, that while I do not get loaves and fishes by my prayer, I get better things—I get virtue, grace, and happiness), that God's blessing may descend and rest upon every one here present, and upon every human being throughout the world.

A vote of thanks was then moved, seconded, and carried by acclamation, to the Umpire and Chairmen, which was briefly acknowledged by Mr. SYME.

APPENDIX.

A.

(*See page* 13.)

ARGUMENTS AND OPINIONS RESPECTING THE EXISTENCE OF A GOD MAINTAINED BY

SOCRATES.

Socrates.—As some things have no character to mark the purpose of their being, while others are obviously made for use, which of these, think you, are works of accident, and which of design?

Aristodemus.—It is clear that things made for use must be works of design.

Socrates.—Does not, then, the Being who first made men, appear also to have given them the several organs of sense for their use—eyes, to see things visible—ears, to hear things audible? Moreover, what good should we have from smells, were nostrils not given us to inhale them? And what perception should we have of things sweet and tart, and of all the pleasures of the palate, had not a tongue been formed within the mouth, to give us a discriminating taste of such matters? To pass on to other examples: think you not, that it looks like the work of prescience, because the sight is delicate, to have guarded it with eyelids, which open when we want to see, but shut when we go to sleep—to have fenced these lids with eyelashes, which, like a sieve, strain the dusty wind, and hinder it from hurting the eyes; and over the eyes to have placed eye-brows, as eaves to carry off the sweat of the brow from disturbing the sight? Again, to have given us ears, capable of taking in all sounds, without being ever crowded by them;—in all animals, to have placed the cutting teeth in front, and the molar teeth behind, fitted to grind down what they have received from the cutting teeth—and near the eyes and nostrils to have placed the mouth, through which the food, each animal delights in, finds an entrance into its body. On the other hand, as the excretions are offensive, to have turned away the ducts by which they escape, and carried them off to the greatest possible distance from the senses; can you doubt, whether organs such as these, framed with so much forethought, are works of chance or of design?

Aristodemus.—No, in very truth, I have no doubt; for in this view, these various organs seem altogether the contrivance of some wise Artificer, who loves the beings he has created.—*Xenophon's Mirabilia*, book i., chap. iv.; and *Sedgwick's Discourse on the Studies of the University of Cambridge*, 5th Edition, pp. 41, and 150—153.

LOCKE.

God, in a clear manifestation of himself amongst them, has laid before them, ever since the creation of the world, his Divine nature and eternal power; so that what is to be known of his invisible Being might be clearly discovered and understood from the visible beauty, order and operations observable in the constitution and parts of the universe, by all those that would cast their regards and apply their minds that way; insomuch that they are utterly without excuse, for that when the Deity was so plainly discovered to them, yet they glorified him not as was suitable to the excellency of his Divine nature, nor did they with due thankfulness acknowledge him as the Author of their being, and the Giver of all the good they enjoyed.—*Locke's Paraphrase on the Epistle of Paul to the Romans*, ch. i., v. 19—21.

HUME.

As every inquiry which regards religion is of the utmost importance, there are two questions in particular which challenge our attention; to wit, that concerning its foundation in reason, and that concerning its origin in human nature. Happily, the first question, which is the most important, admits of the most obvious, at least the clearest solution.

The whole frame of nature bespeaks an intelligent Author; and no rational inquirer can, after serious reflection, suspend his belief a moment with regard to the primary principles of genuine theism and religion.—*Hume's Natural History of Religion.*

Though the stupidity of men, barbarous and uninstructed, be so great, that they may not see a sovereign Author in the more obvious works of nature to which they are so much familiarised; yet it scarcely seems possible that any one of good understanding should reject that idea when once it is suggested to him. A purpose, an intention, a design is evident in everything; and when our comprehension is so far enlarged as to contemplate the first rise of this visible system, we must adopt, with the strongest conviction, the idea of some intelligent cause or author. The uniform maxims, too, which prevail throughout the whole frame of the universe naturally, if not necessarily, lead us to conceive this intelligence as single and individual, where the prejudices of education oppose not so reasonable a theory.—*Ibid.*

The universal propensity to believe in invisible, intelligent power, if not an original, being, at least, an attendant of human nature, may be considered as a kind of mark or stamp which the Divine workman has set upon his work; and nothing surely can more dignify mankind than to be thus selected from all other parts of the creation, and to bear the image or impression of the universal Creator.—*Ibid.*

What a noble privilege is it of human reason to attain the knowledge of the Supreme Being; and, from the visible works of nature, be enabled to infer so sublime a principle as its Supreme Creator.—*Ibid.*

PAINE.

As several of my colleagues, and others of my fellow-citizens of France, have given me the example of making their voluntary and individual profession of faith, I also will make mine, and I do this with all that sincerity and frankness with which the mind of man communicates with itself.

I believe in one God, and no more; and I hope for happiness beyond this life.—*Paine's Age of Reason.*

VOLTAIRE.

We are intelligent beings; and intelligent beings cannot have been formed by a blind, brute, insensible Being; there is certainly some difference between a clod and the ideas of Newton. Newton's intelligence, then, came from some other intelligence.—*Voltaire's Phil. Dict., Art. "Atheism."*

When we see a fine machine, we say there is a good machinist, and that he has an excellent understanding. The world is, assuredly, an admirable machine; therefore there is in the world, somewhere or other, an admirable intelligence. This argument is old, but is not therefore the worse.—*Ibid.*

The members of animals are made for all their necessities with an incomprehensible art; and you have not the boldness to deny it. You mention it not. You feel that you can say nothing in answer to this great argument which nature brings against you. The disposition of the wing of a fly, or of the feelers of a snail, is sufficient to confound you.—*Ibid.*

Unphilosophical geometricians have rejected final causes, but true philosophers admit them; and, as is elsewhere observed, a catechist announces God to children, and Newton demonstrates him to the wise.—*Ibid.*

I should not wish to come in the way of an atheistical prince, whose interest it should be to have me pounded in a mortar. I am quite sure that I should be so pounded. Were I a sovereign, I would not have to do with atheistical courtiers, whose interest it was to poison me: I should be under the necessity of taking an antidote every day. It is, then, absolutely necessary, for princes and people, that the idea of a Supreme Being, creating, governing, and rewarding and punishing, be profoundly engraven on their minds.—*Ibid.*

They say,—Our teachers represent God to us as the most insensate and barbarous of all beings, therefore there is no God. But they ought to say, —Our teachers represent God as furious and ridiculous, therefore God is the reverse of what they describe him. He is as wise and good as they say he is foolish and wicked. Thus do the wise decide.—*Ibid.*

A philosopher was given to the world, who discovered the simple and sublime laws by which the celestial globes move in the immensity of space. Thus the work of the universe, now that it is better known, bespeaks a workman; and so many never-varying laws announce a law-giver. Sound philosophy, therefore, has destroyed atheism, to which obscure theology furnished weapons of defence.—*Ibid.*

I regard true philosophers as the apostles of the Divinity. Each class of men requires its particular ones; a parish catechist tells his children that there is a God, but Newton proves it to the wise. In London, under Charles II., after Cromwell's wars, as at Paris, under Henry IV., after the war of the Guises, people took great pride in being Atheists; having passed from the excess of cruelty to that of pleasure, and corrupted their minds, successively, by war and voluptuousness, they reasoned very indifferently. Since then, the more nature has been studied, the better its Author has been known.—*Ibid.*

The Theist is a man firmly persuaded of the existence of a Supreme Being, equally good and powerful, who has formed all extended vegetation, sentient, and reflecting existences; who perpetuates their species, who punishes crimes without cruelty, and rewards virtuous actions with kindness. The Theist does not know how God punishes, how he rewards, how he pardons; for he is not presumptuous enough to flatter himself that he understands how God acts; but he knows that God does act, and that he is just. The difficulties opposed to a Providence do not stagger him in his faith, because they are only great difficulties, not proofs. He submits himself to that Providence, although he only perceives some of its effects, and some appearances; and judging of the things he does not see from those he does see, he thinks that this Providence pervades all places and all ages.—*Ibid. Art. " Theism."*

Theocracy ought to be universal; for every man, whether a prince or a boatman, should obey the natural and eternal laws which God has given him.—*Ibid.*

ROBESPIERRE.

The idea of a Supreme Being, and of the immortality of the soul, is a continual call to justice; it is, therefore, a social and republican principle. Who has authorised you to declare that the Deity does not exist? Oh, you who support, in such impassioned strains, so arid a doctrine, what advantage do you expect to derive from the principle that a blind fatality regulates the affairs of men, and that the soul is nothing but a breath of air impelled towards the tomb? Will the idea of annihilation inspire man with more pure and elevated sentiments than that of immortality? Will it awaken more respect for others or himself, more courage to resist tyranny, greater contempt for pleasure or death? You who regret a virtuous friend, can you endure the thought that his noblest part has not escaped dissolution? You who weep over the remains of a child or a wife, are you consoled by the thought that a handful of dust is all that remains of the beloved object? You, the unfortunate, who expire under the strokes of an assassin, is not your last voice raised to appeal to the justice of the Most High? Innocence on the scaffold, supported by such thoughts, makes the tyrant turn pale on his triumphal car. Could such an ascendant be felt, if the tomb levelled alike the oppressor and his victim?

Observe how, on all former occasions, tyrants have sought to stifle the idea of the immortality of the soul. With what art did Cæsar, when pleading in the Roman Senate in favour of the accomplices of Catiline, endeavour to throw doubts on the belief of its immortality; while Cicero invokes against the traitor the sword of the laws, and the vengeance of Heaven! Socrates, on the verge of death, discoursed with his friends on the ennobling theme; Leonidas, at Thermopylæ, on the eve of executing the most heroic design ever conceived by man, invited his companions to a banquet in another world. The principles of the Stoics gave birth to Brutus and Cato, even in the ages which witnessed the expiry of Roman virtue; they alone saved the honour of human nature, almost obliterated by the vices and the corruption of the empire. The Encyclopædists contained some estimable characters, but a much greater number of ambitious rascals. Many of them became leading men in the State. Whoever does not study their influence and policy, would form a most imperfect notion of our Revolution. It was they who introduced the frightful doctrine of atheism; they were ever in politics below the dignity of freedom; in morality they went as far beyond the destruction of religious prejudices. Their disciples declaimed against despotism, and received the pensions of despots; they composed alternately tirades against kings, and madrigals for their mistresses; they were fierce with their pens, and rampant in their antechambers. That sect propagated, with infinite care, the principles of Materialism, which spread so rapidly among the great and the *beaux esprits*. We owe to them that selfish philosophy which reduced egotism to a system; regarded human society as a game of chance, where success was the sole distinction between what was just and unjust; probity as an affair of taste or good breeding; the world as the patrimony of the most dexterous scoundrels.—*See Speech made by Robespierre in* 1794, *recorded in Alison's History of Europe*, vol. iv., pp. 224, 225.

B.

(See note q, *p.* 29, *and note* a, *p.* 53.)

If any one admitting that the argument from design goes to establish an *immaterial* Deity, should contend that such Deity has, nevertheless, an *organization*, pleading that the human *mind* is organized, and the human mind being a pattern of the Deity, the Deity must himself be organized also; I answer,—

In the first place,—That there is no organization in the human mind like that which the human body displays. Because,

First, *Separableness is a characteristic of man's corporeal organizations.* The human eye, ear, hand, and foot, *can be separated from one another.* The mental faculties of perception, memory, reason, feeling, and the like, *cannot be separated from one another.*

Secondly, *Divisibility is another characteristic of man's bodily organization.* The *eye* can be not merely separated from the ear, hand, foot, but can itself be divided and subdivided into a countless number of parts. The mental faculty of *perception* is not only incapable of separation from memory, reason, feeling, but also of being itself divided.

If it be asked, Why, then, are man's mental powers spoken of as if they consisted of faculties distinct from one another? It may be answered, that on spiritual and metaphysical subjects, man is not possessed of a complete vocabulary, suited to express the exact ideas intended to be conveyed. That, on such subjects, similes, borrowed from material things, are much employed. Thus, the mind is said to be enlightened, to be darkened, to freeze, to burn, to be hard, to be soft, and the like. Such language, though not with logical exactness expressing the intended ideas, yet is sufficiently intelligible, being rendered so by man's own personal consciousness and experience.

In the second place,—If there were proof of the existence of organization in the human mind, it could not thence be inferred that there must be organization in the Deity also. Because,

First, *The human mind is united to organized matter, but the Deity is distinct from matter altogether.* Where there is so vast a difference as this, to argue that, because the one is organized, the other must be organized also, is to reason without sufficient data.

Secondly, *Because (even upon the supposition that the human mind is organized) limitation is a characteristic of all organic structures.* The functions of man's several *bodily organs* have their limits. The eye cannot hear. The functions of the whole body, regarded as one structure, have a limit. The body cannot fly. The functions of man's several *mental organs* (supposing them, for argument's sake, to be organs) have their limits. The faculty of perception cannot remember. The functions of the whole mind, regarded as one structure, have their limit. They can perform acts only within a limited range. *That the Deity is limited in his functions there is no proof, and there can be no proof. On the contrary, from what the Deity has actually done, reason draws an inference, that there is no work which he is unable to perform.*

If it be objected, that even admitting the Deity to have made the universe, the universe being finite, that would only prove that he possessed finite functions. It is answered, that to prove that God is able to make the universe, is not to prove that he can do nothing more, or that there is any limit to his ability. The reverse is the case. If a Being has made the universe, reason readily infers that there is nothing within the range of possibility which he cannot do.

Mr. Holyoake takes the view, that an *immaterial* Being is necessarily *unorganized*. This is plain from his writings, in which he says, "We cannot conceive of an organized spirit." "All conceivable organizations are material."—*Paley's Natural Theology Refuted*, chap. xi.

J. Unwin, Gresham Steam Press, 31, Bucklersbury, London.